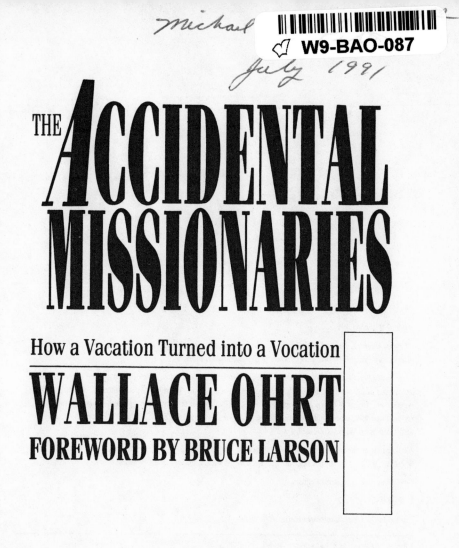

THE *ACCIDENTAL* *MISSIONARIES*

How a Vacation Turned into a Vocation

WALLACE OHRT

FOREWORD BY BRUCE LARSON

INTERVARSITY PRESS
DOWNERS GROVE, ILLINOIS 60515

© 1990 Wallace Ohrt

InterVarsity Press is the book-publishing division of InterVarsity Christian Fellowship, a student movement active on campus at hundreds of universities, colleges and schools of nursing in the United States of America, and a member movement of the International Fellowship of Evangelical Students. For information about local and regional activities, write Public Relations Dept., InterVarsity Christian Fellowship, 6400 Schroeder Rd., P.O. Box 7895, Madison, WI 53707-7895.

All Scripture quotations, unless otherwise indicated, are from the Holy Bible, New International Version. Copyright © 1973, 1978, International Bible Society. Used by permission of Zondervan Bible Publishers.

Cover illustration: Roberta Polfus

ISBN 0-8308-1741-7

Printed in the United States of America ∞

Library of Congress Cataloging-in-Publication Data

Ohrt, Wallace.
    The accidental missionaries: how a vacation turned into a
vocation/by Wallace Ohrt.
      p.   cm.
    ISBN 0-8308-1741-7
    1. Masai (African people)—Missions—Kenya. 2. Grindall, Denny.
3. Grindall, Jeanne. I. Title.
BV3630.M3047   1990
266'.0092'2—dc20
[B]   90-48587
                                      CIP

15	14	13	12	11	10	9	8	7	6	5	4	3	2	1
02	01	00	99	98	97	96	95	94	93	92	91	90		

Foreword

A sign hanging in one of our Sunday-school rooms says: "We don't believe in miracles. We rely on them." Those same words could describe the life and ministry of Denny and Jeanne Grindall.

In a lifetime of traveling, I have met many extraordinary people who have believed in the living presence of Jesus Christ and who have been change agents in the world in the most unlikely places and circumstances. They have been led and empowered by the Holy Spirit literally to work miracles in the lives of others, personally as well as in every level of our corporate lives, neighborhoods, schools, businesses and governments. Those people belong to the kingdom of priests that God has dreamed about from the beginning (Ex 19:6), the royal priesthood of the New Testament. This ministry of the laity is the final product, or bottom line, of the church. It is those men and women who are the salt, light and leaven of which Jesus spoke.

Well, this book is about the two most extraordinary lay ministers I have ever known. They walk right out of the pages of the New Testament and into the hearts of the Maasai tribes of Kenya. Those beautiful people of the Rift Valley of Africa will never again be the same.

This perceptively written book faithfully chronicles how those

astounding twenty years in Denny's and Jeanne's efforts changed a
nation. To some, the Grindalls' effectiveness seems puzzling. They
have no formal training to be missionaries—no university or seminary degree in how to work and live in a Third World setting. But,
like the first-century Christians, they have an abiding faith in Jesus
as Lord, and they know how to love people as friends, not objects
of charity. Most of all, they rely on the Holy Spirit to create miracles.

It is my hope that this book will be widely read by all kinds of
people. Denny and Jeanne are the best role models I know for
Christians who want to live out their faith in a hurting world. As
for non-Christians, this story captures, as few others do, the adventure and fulfillment of life as it was meant to be lived.

Bruce Larson

Preface

Some years ago, our church offered a Sunday-night program featuring Denny and Jeanne Grindall, a Seattle couple who were doing some interesting work among the Maasai people of Kenya. Their slide presentation sparked in me a lasting interest that gnawed at my literary vitals until I found a way to meet and persuade the Grindalls to allow me to tell their story in book form.

It has been a fascinating experience that has provided many rewards. I have acquired two wonderfully interesting, loving friends. I have fulfilled a lifelong ambition to travel in Africa. I have come to know the Maasai people and learn something of their rich but little-known history and culture. Best of all, I have been privileged to witness the results of an authentic miracle that God wrought in Kenya.

The Grindalls have never thought of themselves as missionaries, but rather as friends and neighbors of the villagers of the Olosho-Oibor district, even though their own neighborhood in Suquamish, Washington, is on the other side of the world. Nevertheless, they have shared a fate common to many missionaries: having their motives misunderstood and their efforts criticized by some onlookers and visitors. In their case, the criticism may even have been more than ordinarily harsh because of the glamorous image of the

Maasai and the universal admiration in which they are held. Why disrupt the simple lifestyle of these attractive and seemingly contented people? After all, can we be sure that our ways are so much better than theirs?

The Maasai are nomadic herdsmen of cattle, goats and sheep, wandering over great distances in search of water and grass when the irregular East African rains fail. With the onrush of "progress" cutting off their traditional routes, they find life increasingly difficult, especially in times of prolonged drought. Those who object to "interference" with the traditional way of life fail to take into account the extreme fragility of that way. But others, even the Maasai scholar Tepilit ole Saitori, recognize, albeit sadly, that the Maasai must adapt to the modern world or cease to exist as a people. Denny and Jeanne also sensed this poignant reality from their first visit as tourists. They devoted a major portion of their lives to helping the Maasai make the inevitable transition.

What followed is as much the story of Samuel Pulei, Chief Simeon, Jonah and the other people of Olosho-Oibor as that of the Grindalls. It was these visionary Maasai leaders who convinced their neighbors to deviate from long-cherished traditions in order to give their children a more stable, healthy way of life. The crosscultural communication barriers were formidable, and some mistakes and misunderstandings inevitably occurred. One of the clearest proofs that God's hand was on their adventure is seen in that all differences were reconciled and all antagonisms resolved. Nevertheless, to preclude the reopening of old wounds, the Grindalls have requested that several names be disguised. These few pseudonyms are indicated by footnotes. They in no way alter the factual nature of the account.

The reader may ask why the Grindalls have authorized the telling of their story now at the risk of even the slightest injury to their

African friends. The answer comes promptly from Denny.

We think there are many American Christians, especially vigorous early retirees, who have skills and resources that could, if
properly put to use, help to heal a hurting world. We want to
encourage them to try. We don't claim that our own experience
is a model; there are probably many better ways than ours. After
all, I'm a florist, not an engineer, and Jeanne is a homemaker. If
we, with God's help, could make some small difference, others
can too.

One
UNKNOWN DESTINIES
1934

Great Rift Valley,
Kenya, East Africa

In the near-total darkness, Endorop sensed rather than saw that another person had entered her hovel. Then, dimly, she recognized her neighbor. The woman approached and extended her hands, palms up, in a gesture of command. Endorop moaned and clutched the child in her arms protectively.

"Give him to me," said the intruder. Her tone was firm but not harsh. "The elders have held council. The child must be taken out now, before the sun is gone."

The tensely crouching Endorop began to rock back and forth rhythmically in silent despair.

"Do not be foolish," said the other woman brusquely. "Anyone can see that he will not live through the night. If he dies here, disaster will fall upon the whole village. Engai Na-Nyokie will punish us all, and your house will have to be purged."

Dully, Endorop acknowledged to herself the truth of these words. For a corpse to remain, even for a moment, in the presence of living beings would be a calamity. The resultant pollution would require a fearful cleansing, a ritual that filled her with fear. A hole would be knocked in the wall of her house. Then a trail of putrid animal entrails would be dragged from that hole through an opening in the barricade of thornbrush surrounding the village, an invitation to the hyenas to enter and remove the offending body.

Numbly, she ceased her rocking. Sensing her surrender, the other woman said more gently, "Now you are sensible. There is nothing to be gained by being beaten for obstinacy. It will come to the same thing anyway."

She took the inert form, astonishingly light and fragile, from the mother's hands. "May Engai give you other sons," she murmured, departing as silently as she had entered.

A group of elders waited outside. They nodded in satisfaction as the woman approached with the fever-racked infant. Norombo, the grizzled chief, took the child and, with the other elders following, walked slowly to a large acacia tree on a low rise several hundred yards away. One of the elders spread a calfskin on the ground beneath the tree. On this the chief placed the child, cushioning the tiny head on the folded left arm with the face directed toward the place where the sun would rise over the Ngong Hills. A faint sigh escaped the infant's cracked lips; otherwise there was no sign of life. The elders nodded in satisfaction; they had won the race with death and so were spared the necessity of ritual purging.

As the elders prepared to depart, two tall young warriors in full battle regalia arrived and stationed themselves flanking the acacia tree. Each wore his hair plaited in long braids interwoven with strands of wool and cut square midway between shoulder and waist. Each man's hair, ears and face were coated with red ocher mixed with sheep fat. His long legs were painted with *entoroto,* a chalky substance that had been intricately patterned with fingernail tracings to expose the darker skin beneath. A short sword in a leather scabbard was attached to a thin, beaded belt around each lean waist. A thigh bell, fastened at belt and knee, tinkled with each warrior's movements. Each man held his broad-blade Maasai stabbing spear close to his body. The senior, identifiable by the opulence of his amulets, ear ornaments, necklaces and ankle chains, carried a short bow slung over one shoulder and a half dozen blunt arrows in a quiver at his waist. Despite these lavish accoutrements, each man wore only a single garment: a sketchy charcoal-darkened toga secured at the throat and fluttering open in the steady Rift Valley wind to expose the wearer's athletic body.

The two warriors took no notice of the departing elders. Their *moran* code required them to be oblivious to all but themselves unless danger was present. The only duty of morans being the protection of Maasai life and property, the task facing these two was simply to stand guard over the dying infant to spare it from being eaten by despised birds. With sunset, all birds would fly to their nests; then the two guards would return to their warrior *manyatta* for the night, leaving the body, whether still living or dead, for the honored hyenas.

Toward sundown a lone vulture swooped low. The two warriors gave no sign that they were aware of the obscene presence, but the bird quickly recognized its danger. With a thrust of its powerful pinions it soared aloft and vanished in the gathering dusk. With the sun's descent behind the hills, the long shadows swiftly blended into darkness. Where a moment earlier the warriors stood forth clearly, now they appeared as featureless silhouettes against the glowing sky. By unspoken assent, they lifted their spears and broke into a jog trot, leaving only the lone tree to guard the tiny figure on the calfskin.

Next morning Norombo dispatched one of his sons to the acacia tree to recover the calfskin. Soon the boy returned empty-handed. The chief frowned.

"Have the greedy, thieving hyenas taken the funeral robe?" he demanded. "No, father," said the youth. "The hyenas did not come." Norombo immediately convened the elders. "Our offering has been refused," he told them. "Perhaps it was too meager a meal. Or maybe the scent was too faint to catch the night wind. We must be sure we do not fail again and bring disgrace on our village. The departed one was Senteu's kin; therefore, it is for Senteu to make matters right."

Senteu rose and went out to a nearby herd of grazing goats. Selecting a black male, he fastened a cord about its neck and led it to a fire pit near the funeral tree. After asking its pardon, he smothered it by clamping a hand over its slender muzzle. He then skinned the animal and soon had it roasting over a charcoal fire. As the rich aroma of cooking meat spread, the fat bubbled and dripped. The watching elders nodded approval.

"The hyenas will come tonight," predicted the chief. "Let us make sure they do their work well this time."

With a wooden bowl he collected a quantity of dripping fat, which he took to the small form huddled under the acacia tree. The position of the body was unchanged since the previous evening. Satisfied that life had departed, Norombo dipped his hand into the bowl and began to spread the goat fat on the infant's body, but abruptly he paused, frowning. Again he began to anoint the body, but again he drew back his hand, almost in fear. He stood up slowly. "We must not do this thing," he muttered. "The child is still warm!"

Engai has chosen to keep it alive!"

Two days later, although the infant remained comatose, its breathing was audible. It even sucked a few drops of goat's milk from Endorop's fingers. The villagers became nervous about the delicate balance between life and death. "We must send for the laibon," announced the chief. "He will know what to do."

The laibon arrived in mid-afternoon. He was an imposing figure encased in a long cape of hyrax skins. His wide-set, hooded eyes stared fixedly from deep sockets. Endorop's listless infant was brought before him.

"The child will neither live nor die," complained Norombo. He recounted the procedure that had been followed. The medicine man listened impassively, then laid a wrinkled hand on the child's hot skin.

"Evil spirits dwell in him," he intoned. "Until they are driven out, he will not recover."

From the folds of his hyrax cape he produced a pouch of goat-skin, which he unrolled ceremoniously. The elders watched in awe as he drew forth a lancet of sharpened bone.

"This is no ordinary evil spirit," he informed them. "If it were, I could drive it out of the child's mouth, but for this one I must make another way of escape."

He grasped a pinch of skin below the collarbone and plunged the lancet through, creating two puncture wounds with a single thrust.

A squall of fury burst from the baby, who clenched his tiny fists and kicked his feet in the air mightily. As blood spurted from the twin incisions, the cries grew still louder and more indignant. The medicine man nodded in satisfaction.

"The evil one has fled. The child will recover now." He regarded the bellowing, kicking infant with wonder. "Surely Engai must have a great plan in store for this one," he muttered.

Seattle, Washington

With varying degrees of interest, the members of the history class at Roosevelt High School in Washington State followed the discussion led by their teacher about the history of their state. She occasionally touched the wall map behind her with a pointer.

"In February of 1852, Mr. Bell, Mr. Boren and the Denny brothers located claims on the east side of Elliott Bay. Others soon followed, and in May of 1853 Mr. Boren and Arthur Denny filed the first plat of the town that was to be named after the Indian chief Sealth, whose name was as hard for the early settlers to pronounce as it is for us."

A sandy-haired youth in the far corner of the classroom was so intent on a nearby building project where workmen were erecting a red-brick apartment house that at first he did not hear his name called. He was fascinated by the teamwork of the different craftsmen as they integrated their skills into the total operation. The bricklayers on their scaffolds did not have to call for bricks or mortar; their materials were delivered to their work platforms by a crane that swung its dangling bucket as gracefully as a spider spinning a web.

"Denny Grindall!" the teacher said sharply. "Are you with us today?"

With a start but with no apparent embarrassment, the sandy-haired boy flashed an infectious smile, against which the teacher's annoyance melted.

"Yes, ma'am. Would you please repeat the question?"

"Can you tell us who filed the second city plat, following the one filed by Mr. Boren and your eminent ancestor?"

"He was a relative but not really my ancestor," the youth corrected her. "Arthur Denny was my grandfather's cousin. And the answer to the question is Doc Maynard. He built a salmon packing plant. Then he sold off the rest of his land for use as business lots. My mother used to tell us about old Doc."

The teacher nodded approval. "Very good, Denny."

When the class bell signalled the end of the hour and the students filed out, the teacher detained the sandy-haired youth.

"Denny," she said gently, "I get the feeling that Washington State history doesn't interest you very much."

Again came the flashing smile. "I guess you're right," he admitted cheerfully.

Taken aback by his unexpected candor, she asked, "What about your other classes? Do any of them interest you?"

"No, I can't say they do. I guess I'm not really much of a student."

Still perplexed, she pressed on. "Then what does interest you, Denny? What were you studying so intently when I called on you?"

"I was watching that construction project down the street. I was thinking I'd like to have some of that cement to build a boat."

The teacher frowned. "A boat made of cement? I should think it would sink."

"Oh, no, ma'am. Ferro-cement boats are very seaworthy."

"Ferro-cement?" she echoed.

"That's right. It's really concrete reinforced with steel mesh. It makes a strong, rigid hull without too much thickness or weight."

"That's very interesting, Denny. Are you planning to manufacture boats when you graduate?"

"No, ma'am, but I do plan to go into the merchant marine service."

"Indeed? And will you make that your career?"

"No, I just want to see the world for a couple of years; then I'm going to settle down and go into some kind of business for myself."

"Well, I'm sure you will succeed at whatever you do, but I recommend that you apply yourself more seriously to your studies in the few remaining months you will be in high school. You must be sure to graduate, because that will be important if you are going into business. Don't waste this precious time looking out the window, Denny."

Chastened, Denny grinned ruefully. "I'm sure you're right, ma'am, and I'll try to do what you say. Now may I leave? I have a job after school, and I don't want to be late."

With a reassuring smile, she gave his freckled hand a squeeze. "Of course you may. Run along, Denny. And good luck with those great plans."

Two
A TROUBLED
YOUTH
1946

Senteu stood beneath a flat-crowned acacia tree, surveying his cattle and contemplating the state of his personal affairs. In other circumstances he would have taken much satisfaction in both. A senior elder these past four years, he now possessed three wives and was considering taking a fourth soon. He also had many children; his wives could furnish the exact number, should it ever become important for him to know. Concerning livestock his knowledge was precise: he owned forty-two heifers, eighteen bullocks, twenty calves and yearlings and two fine bulls; of goats, he claimed eighty, plus seventy-two fat-tailed sheep. Engai had been generous.

Still there was cause for worry. As he shaded his eyes with his hand and scanned the rangeland with an experienced eye, he saw only scattered clumps of dry, sparse lion grass where, at this season, there should be a waving carpet of green to the distant horizon. For nearly a year scarcely any rain had fallen. The ribs of the cattle stuck out from their shrunken hides like sticks in a mud wall. Their plaintive bellows distressed him sorely. If rain did not come soon, he would have to drive his herds into the highlands in search of better grass, which would be found only if springs or streams still flowed there. The decision would not be made easily, even for one of Senteu's long nomadic background. There would be much hard work for the womenfolk: collecting wattles, mud and dung to build huts, and erecting thornbrush enclosures for the protection of humans and animals. But it was not the labor problem of women that troubled Senteu; his thoughts were on the hungry leopards that would be prowling those hills, stalking the shrinking waterholes for domestic animals whose thirst would overcome caution. He knew he could not count on the morans to guard his herds, for the entire clan would be scattered across the highland, seeking grass and water like himself. The warriors would not be able to protect them all.

On a low hill a quarter mile away his nephew and ward Ntienput stood watch over Senteu's sheep, his legs crossed in typical Maasai herdboy stance with three cattle sticks, varying in length according to tradition, clamped between his thighs. The boy was more like a son than a nephew, for his father, Senteu's brother, had died twelve years ago while Ntienput was still in his mother's womb. There was a soberness, a seriousness, in the boy that his guardian found troubling, for Senteu believed that every Maasai youth should be lighthearted and carefree. He studied the lad critically, thinking him a trifle small for his age. Perhaps in the three or four years before circumcision, he would grow to a warrior's stature. Senteu raised his hand in a beckoning gesture. Senteu studied the approaching youth, reassuring himself with the thought that Ntienput's close brush with death in infancy could have left its mark on him. If so, he might yet outgrow the evil influence and become like the other young males, but now he seemed to have none of the healthy impatience of a normal Maasai boy to become a moran, live in the manyatta with his peers and enjoy all the glories of that estate. He did not follow the warriors around, aping their vain mannerisms and sneaking lustful glances at their girlfriends as young boys were expected to do. He had not even asked to have wooden plugs inserted in his earlobes to stretch the holes in preparation for the elaborate ornamentation that would follow circumcision. To Senteu, the boy's behavior was unnatural.

As Ntienput approached his uncle, he inclined his head and lowered his eyes in the customary greeting of child to adult. Senteu placed his hand briefly on the close-cropped head, though the exchange was a trifle more formal than custom required between members of the same household.

"You seem troubled, nephew. Has a sheep strayed? Are your insides giving you pain?"

"No, uncle." The boy's tone was listless, and he did not raise his eyes.

"What, then? Has a cheetah bitten off your tongue?"

Ntienput sighed. "I am lonely for my friend Ngeshu. I miss him greatly."

Senteu grunted disdainfully. "That one whose father sent him to the missionary school, is it? Hah! A foolish father deserves a foolish son. Ngeshu would do better tending his father's goats and learning useful things."

"He is learning to read and write," the boy said defensively.

"What need has a Maasai for learning?" Senteu snorted. "Will the little bird tracks on paper make the rain fall or drive away the lioness? Of course not! An educated Maasai is a lost person, useless to his people, for he is cut off from the traditions that sustain us."

The boy kept his eyes lowered, avoiding his uncle's indignant scowl. At length, with great effort, he said, "Uncle, I myself have learned to read a little. I would like to learn more."

Senteu was dumbfounded. "What is this? My own nephew desires to follow bird tracks on a piece of paper? How did this thing come to be?"

Reluctantly, the boy said, "There was a man who came here from a far place called Narok. . . ."

"Lakashu!" Senteu spat out the name like a curse. "The learned one who took advantage of our hospitality to make big wind about things of no interest or importance. A starving jackal, useless as a barren ewe! What passed between you and Lakashu?"

Daunted by his uncle's wrath, Ntienput was slow to answer. "One day I watched him," he said hesitantly, "wondering what the thing was that he held in his hands and stared at with much interest. He saw me watching and motioned for me to come near. I saw then that when his eyes followed the little tracks on the thing in his hands and he spoke familiar words, he got the words from the tracks. They didn't come from his head. He called the thing *a book* and said he would teach me to gather words from it. Each night I went to his hut, and he showed me how to follow the little tracks."

Avoiding his uncle's eye, Ntienput plunged ahead. "One day Lakashu said he would show me how to make the tracks that speak my name. Like this."

With the longest of his three cattle sticks he traced the letters *NTIENPUT* in the dust.

Angrily, Senteu kicked the marks away. "Worthless one! Better the hyenas had eaten you when you were no higher than a goat's udder, when we thought you were dead, as you should have been!"

The youth remained silent as his uncle glared at him. Gradually the man's anger abated, and he resumed speaking, this time more calmly.

"Consider carefully what I have to say. It is well known that of all people, the Maasai are most favored by Engai. The life of a Maasi man is divided into four parts of about equal length if he lives to enjoy them all. First, he is a child, as you are now, and he plays children's games until he is old enough to herd goats and sheep. Later he is circumcised and becomes a moran. That is the time of joy, the dream of every youth. A moran is envied by younger boys, loved by many girls and admired by his clan. He has pride in himself and is the pride of his parents. He lives with his comrades, and his only duty is to protect the clan. He is the slayer of lions, the bold, laughing Maasai warrior. Nowhere is there anyone who can stand against him.

"Later, he becomes an elder, a man of substance and wisdom and responsibility. He acquires wives and children, cattle, and many sheep and goats. He shares in the council with the other elders. At the time of Olngesherr, when he is confirmed in full elderhood, he drinks the ceremonial honey beer and sacrifices a fine bullock to Engai. But even if he becomes rich and powerful and respected, he will not again know the joy and freedom he knew as a moran.

"And last of all, if Engai extends his days, he becomes an ancient elder. He wraps himself in his warm blanket and sits apart under a tree with his fly whisk and cattle stick, dreaming of the lions he has killed and the maidens he has known. Even though he is no longer powerful in the elders' councils, he is loved by the children and venerated as a storyteller.

"All these passages are sweet and good, but only for those who enter fully into the Maasai way of life. You, who have not even completed the first stage, talk foolishly of books and learning. I tell you solemnly, nephew, education only leads to the ruin of a Maasai."

Ntienput shifted his feet uneasily. At length he said diffidently, "Will my uncle permit me to speak?"

Senteu scowled. "Speak, then, but be careful what you say."

The boy stooped and plucked a handful of dry grass. "All depends on this," he said. "When it is tender and green and plentiful, our cows grow fat and their udders are full. When it is brown and dead, like now, they bellow in pain and we starve. I think there must be a way to live without always having to watch for passing clouds."

Senteu raised his stick as if to strike the boy. With an effort he stayed his arm, but his words rained down like blows.

"A child who does not heed the words of his elders is worthless! You do not deserve to be a Maasai! My words are not dry dung blowing in the wind! If you do not respect and obey what I tell you, I will cast you out to the hyenas. Then they can do to you what they should have done long ago."

Three
BREAKING AWAY
1948

The coming of the sun each day was no longer a benediction but a curse. Its malignant glare, revealing the devastation of a two-year drought, threatened another day of torment. Dead trees loomed like gallows on the cracked, parched plain. Mummified carcasses of cattle, sheep and goats littered the ground. Here and there a few gaunt animals tottered and lurched about in search of the few remaining tufts of grass. They were the remnants of the once flourishing Maasai herds. Most of the other survivors had been driven into the highlands, where a few precious drops still seeped from the rocks.

Silence gripped the village, where in better times the children had played noisily and women had mended mud-walled hovels with fresh dung. Those with strength enough to travel had gone into the hills with the cattle; the others waited in their houses for rain or death.

The widow, Endorop, was one of the latter. Her grown sons no longer lived with her; they roamed with the morans and slept in the warrior manyatta. Her younger children, lacking milk, had not survived the drought. Only Ntienput, now fourteen, remained to comfort her. She saw him standing in the darkness before her, and an intuitive dread gripped her.

"You are going away," she said faintly. It was not a question but a statement.

"Yes, mother. I came to say goodbye."

"Where will you go? How will you live . . . an uncircumcised youth?"

"I can't live here. The food is gone. The water holes are like fire pits. The cows and goats, the few that still live, have only dust in their udders."

"Have you spoken of this to your uncle?"

"No, he would not allow me to go. When I am gone, though, he will have one less to feed."

Endorop enfolded her thin body with her arms and made soft sounds of woe. Presently she asked, "Will I ever see you again?"

"Yes, mother. I will return, but not soon. My uncle must have time for his anger to cool." He was silent for a time; then he said quietly, "I don't know where I will go or what I will do. I only know that somewhere there must be a better way to live than our way."

Endorop's response was so long in coming that her son wondered if she had heard him. Then, in a voice barely above a whisper, she said, "Go, then, and find it." Huskily, she added, "And when you do find it, don't forget your people."

"I won't. I promise."

"I have no gift to give you . . . only this." She slipped the shuka from her thin shoulders and held it out to him.

"No," he protested. "I can't take the garment from your back."

"Take it," she insisted. "The nights will be cold. If you are to find what you seek, you must stay alive."

With great reluctance, he took the woolen cloak.

"Now go," she said, "before your uncle learns of this."

Trudging along the stony path, Ntienput reflected on the seriousness of his action. Once, two years ago, his uncle had threatened to cast him out of the village; now he was an outcast by his own action. He knew he would never again be welcome in a Maasai village, for a child's rebellion was a serious offense. A more immediate problem confronted him. He did not know where the path that he followed led. He had no experience of any place beyond the hills on one side and the towering escarpment of the Rift on the other. He had learned that these were boundaries beyond which no Maasai could travel. They were the finite limits of his universe, yet strangers sometimes entered this sealed world from distant places. Lakashu, who had taught him the rudiments of reading, was one of these. He assumed, dimly, that there must be some way out.

Above the Ngong Hills hung a thin crescent moon, plainly visible even in sunlight. Studying it, he thought of the ancient legend he had heard so often by firelight after the animals had been bedded down within the thorn enclosure. According to this tale, Leeyo, father of the Maasai tribe, once received from Engai the offer of immortality for himself and his people. Engai instructed Leeyo to cast away the body of the next child to die in his village while intoning these words:

Man, die and come back again.

Moon, die and stay away.

By these words, Leeyo would sacrifice forever the moon's blessed light. He would gain, in exchange, life without end for himself and his people.

Not long after this revelation, a child died in the village. Leeyo thought of the divine instruction he had received, but the child was not his, and moonlight streamed across the hills with unreal beauty. Leeyo could not bear to give up forever the blessing of its silver beam. He took the dead child out of the thornbrush enclosure and, holding it high, cried out.

Leeyo had scarcely returned to his hut when a child's agonized cry froze his heart with fear. The sound came from the mat at his side where his own beloved son lay, and when Leeyo embraced him, the child convulsed and died in his arms. Leeyo again rushed forth and, holding his dead son high, called out:

Man, die and come back again.

Moon, die and stay away.

But it was no use. Sternly, Engai reminded him of the divine conditions. Then he declared that Leeyo's lack of concern for the first child had cost him and his tribe the promised immortality. As consolation, Engai promised to revive the dead moon at regular intervals.

The old legend charmed and haunted Ntienput, but he had always sensed that it was only a story. Most other children of the village believed without question all the puzzling things their parents told them. Ntienput, however, had developed an early discernment of what was credible and what was not.

The sun, now directly overhead, beat down on the traveler with pitiless intensity. He sank gratefully under a euphorbia candelabra tree, which cast only meager shade but had survived the drought better than the leafier trees in the area. From a goatskin pouch at his waist he took some small scraps of mutton, which he chewed slowly. From the same pouch he took a soiled and tattered booklet and began studying it as he ate. It had come into his possession in a strange way and was a major reason for his departure from the village of his people.

Several months ago, a wandering evangelist had come to his village. The elders listened politely to what the stranger told them, but when some boys edged close to listen, the men drove them away with scowls and threatening gestures. Such ideas were not for the ears of children. Noting this, the evangelist quietly distributed some of his tracts among the boys before leaving the village. Most of the children soon lost interest, but Ntienput, recalling Lakashu's instruction and recognizing some of the curious symbols, hid and kept his copy. He studied the pamphlet as he rested under the euphorbia tree.

The little book included not only rows of the strange bird tracks, the meaning of which Ntienput had begun to discover under Lakashu's tutelage, but also a figure drawn in the likeness of a human being . . . something he had never seen before. The face and hands of the figure were oddly pale, and the slender form was clothed in a long robe. He concluded that the being depicted must be a woman, perhaps an albino, though he couldn't be certain. He pored over the strange image and accompanying symbols.

The process was very laborious, yet somehow the effort seemed worthwhile. He concluded that the bird-track writings related somehow to the image of the human being, delineating and describing the person; therefore, the person must be important. If, indeed, the figure was female, this conclusion contradicted all that he had learned about the worthlessness of that gender, for the words that he laboriously pieced together conveyed the opposite impression. Was she perhaps a *laibon* . . . a wizard? It seemed unlikely; he had never heard of a female laibon. Moreover, if he understood the bird tracks' meaning, this person possessed power and prestige exceeding even a laibon's. It was all quite baffling, yet strangely stirring. Realizing with a start that the sun had moved far to the west, he put the pamphlet away carefully and turned his steps again to the steeply climbing path.

At the Ololua Primary School in the town of Ngong, a tall Englishman thoughtfully stroked his beard as he studied the dusty youth in the soiled shuka who stood silently before him.

"Are you sure he is a Maasai?" the White man asked dubiously. "He seems rather darker than most of them, and he doesn't have holes in his ears."

"Quite sure," asserted the short, gray-haired woman to whom the question was addressed. "I know a bit of their language. I couldn't be mistaken."

"Deucedly odd," muttered the headmaster. "What do you suppose he wants?"

"I think he wants to enroll, sir."

"Astonishing! Most Maasai hate the very thought of education. Also, this presents some problems. You are the only one here who speaks his language, and I'm sure you'll agree you are not fluent in Maa. And, of course, he has no English or Swahili. How would we teach him? How does he propose to take care of his tuition?"

"He made signs suggesting that if we will teach him, he will work."

"Well, it's all very irregular, and a bit risky too. Most of them are quite ferocious. Also, from what I know of them, Maasai males don't work, unless you allow that standing on one leg while watching cows graze can be considered work. What is your recommendation?"

"This one doesn't seem much like the others I've seen. I think we might possibly take a chance on him."

"Very well then, but he's your protege, Miss Hawley. I'll find some chores for him to do, and we'll see if this noble savage is really a scholar in disguise. By the by, what does he call himself?"

"As nearly as I can make out," said Miss Hawley, "his name is Ntienput."

* * *

It is widely acknowledged that University Presbyterian Church in Seattle, Washington, is a vital institution that takes its many ministries seriously. This large, urban church has for many years enjoyed dynamic, visionary leadership and a group of dedicated lay people. They strive earnestly to carry out the Lord's command: "Go into all the world and preach the good news to all creation" (Mk 16:15). With its distinguished pastoral staff, central location and active congregation, UPC has always grown, so steadily in fact that in recent years it has adopted a policy of dividing itself and sending members to join and revitalize languishing neighbor churches. However, during the early postwar period with which this chapter is concerned, UPC dealt with growth in much the same way as other churches. It simply built more buildings on its own church campus.

Dr. David Cowie came to UPC as senior pastor in 1947. A young man of thirty-five, he had already established a reputation as a church builder. His passion, next to swelling the ranks of the saints, was the development of superb facilities for worship, study and fellowship. Soon after his arrival, the session proposed and the congregation approved an ambitious expansion program. To keep costs down, Dr. Cowie appealed to the congregation for help from those having the requisite skills and tools to accomplish the job. The response was gratifying both in number and qualifications of the volunteers. One who answered the call was Denny Grindall, a young businessman recently ordained as an elder.

In 1940 Denny Grindall had married his youthful sweetheart, Jeanne Ward. With his own hands, he built their honeymoon cottage on a portion of the historic homestead of Seattle pioneers John and Mary Denny. His mother, who before her marriage was Loretta

Denny, had inherited part of the old property. After her death her husband apportioned the property as building lots to each of their three children: Grace, Denny and Phyllis.

Denny and Jeanne received the two-acre plot as a wedding present. At the time, Denny's job as outside salesman for a seed company took him to many places in western Washington State, affording opportunities to fulfill his strong entrepreneurial drive. In 1942 he borrowed money to purchase a distressed seed and pet store not far from his home. By 1945 he was able to build the business up and sell it profitably, thus financing a new enterprise, the Aurora Flower Shop and Nursery Greenhouse, a mile east of the old feed store.

During these busy years, three children arrived: daughter Jacquelyn and sons Stephen and Paul. With the expense of a growing family added to the cost of running a business, nearly everything the hard-pressed young couple accomplished during those years had to be achieved by their own labor. Jeanne doubled as mother and storekeeper while Denny became a self-taught carpenter, plumber, electrician and cement finisher as well as nurseryman and manager. Often, when weariness overwhelmed him, he envied others who could afford to hire those services. Today, though, Denny believes that the Lord was preparing him for more demanding tasks to come. At the time he knew only weariness and struggle.

By general agreement, the volunteer crew worked at the church through the evening hours after early dinner. Dr. Cowie, who was himself a skilled and versatile craftsman, arrived on the job first and was always last to leave. He had a gift for making fun out of work, both for himself and for his crew. He regularly provided refreshments, and the men looked forward eagerly to each evening's break for snacks. Late one evening as the crew paused for donuts and coffee, Dr. Cowie spoke thoughtfully.

"You know, men, this is a wonderful thing you are doing. Soon this beautiful new building will ring with music and laughter. Voices will be raised here in prayer and praise. Many a young couple will start out here on their journey of marriage. Little children will learn in these classrooms that Jesus loves them. Bible classes will strengthen people's knowledge and faith."

The faces of the listeners glowed with appreciation of the young pastor's words. When he resumed speaking, his voice and manner were somber.

"But let me tell you something, fellows. There is a suffering world out beyond these walls, and until Christians are willing to leave their safe and cozy home churches and go do something about it, that hurting world will go right on suffering." It was nearly midnight when Denny parked in the driveway and entered the house by the side door to the kitchen where Jeanne was waiting up for him. By long habit, they talked softly to avoid waking the children. Denny recounted Dr. Cowie's prophetic words to Jeanne.

"You know, honey," he said thoughtfully, "I was beginning to feel kind of proud of myself for putting in all these hours at the church. I guess I felt like I was earning another star for my crown. Now I'm not so sure. Maybe being a Christian is a lot harder than I thought."

"Too hard, dear?" There was the hint of a smile in her voice.

He stood up and stretched his aching muscles, answering her smile with a rueful grin. "I hope not, but I'll tell you one thing: That preacher's words sure bored into me. Wish I knew why."

Four
NEW FRIENDS
1968

Success had crowned the Grindalls' years of hard work. The florist and greenhouse business had flourished and expanded. Their children were grown: Jackie and Paul were happily married and Steve was in dental school. For several years Denny and Jeanne had enjoyed annual vacation voyages in tramp steamers to distant, romantic parts of the world. Now they were looking forward to another trip . . . the most ambitious to date. On Sunday, as they were leaving church, Senior Pastor Robert Munger greeted them at the door.

"What's this I hear about you two going on another trip? Where to this time?"

"We're going big-game hunting in East Africa," Denny said.

The pastor's expression betrayed astonishment. "Really? I guess

I wasn't aware you are trophy hunters."

"Oh, yes," said Denny, still deadpan. "You see, Jeanne gave me a thirty-five-millimeter camera, so now I have to find something to shoot."

"I see," said Munger with obvious relief. "When do you leave?"

"We sail Tuesday morning on the *African Meteor.*"

"So soon? I'd hoped to get a word with you before you leave. This may be my last opportunity. Do you mind waiting for me in the foyer?"

Slightly mystified, they acceded to the request and then accompanied the pastor to his office.

"What inspired this adventure?" inquired the tall, gray-haired clergyman as his guests settled themselves into comfortable chairs.

Between them, they recounted how, the previous year during a steamer cruise to South America, they had spent an evening ashore in a Chilean seaport. While exchanging impressions with their fellow passengers as they lounged before a crackling fire in their hotel, the Grindalls marveled over the thrilling experiences their cruise was affording them. A tiny old woman, frail as a twig, smiled at their enthusiastic comments.

"You have seen nothing, my dears," she said, "until you have been to Kenya and seen fifty elephants moving single file beside you."

"That settled it for us," said Denny. "We have to see those animals."

Dr. Munger nodded appreciatively. "I'm sure you're wondering what all this is about. You see, some dear old friends of mine are starting a new ministry in Kenya after being kicked out of Sudan. Their names are Margaret and Lowrie Anderson. I was hoping you might look them up and convey our love."

The Grindalls' faces expressed uncertainty. Then Denny responded cautiously. "That's a good idea, pastor, but won't they be hard to find? You know, Kenya is almost as big as Texas."

Dr. Munger smiled. "They are in Nairobi, where I'm sure your party will spend some time. I can't give you their address, but I can direct you to another couple, the Carmichaels, who are bound to know how to locate them."

"We can try, but I don't promise we can make contact with them," said Denny. "We'll be traveling with a group, you know, and these tour itineraries are pretty tight."

Dr. Munger nodded. "Of course. I quite understand. But you will do your best, won't you? I'm sure you won't regret it; they're a grand old couple."

After an exciting two-week tour of Kenya's game parks, the Grindalls said goodbye to their safari mates in Nairobi. They still had several free days before their steamer's scheduled departure from Mombasa, some three hundred miles away.

On a fine, clear Sunday morning Jeanne placed a call from their hotel, the stately old Norfolk, to the Carmichaels. A warm male voice answered. Mr. Carmichael was delighted to hear from Americans. He assured Jeanne that he did indeed know the Andersons and would be delighted to take the visitors to their house; however, he and his wife were about to leave for church. Would the Grindalls care to meet them there and proceed after the service to the Andersons?

This arrangement being quickly agreed upon, Carmichael gave directions to a Baptist church on Ngong Avenue. He added with a chuckle, "I must warn you that Ngong is a popular place name here. Ngong Avenue angles off Ngong Road, which intersects Kenyatta Avenue, just a few blocks from your hotel. I hope that isn't too confusing."

They found Ngong Road without difficulty and soon came to First Ngong Avenue, which they followed a goodly distance to its end without discovering a Baptist church. Puzzled, but knowing nothing else to do, they returned to Ngong Road and proceeded along it to the next side street, which proved to be Second Ngong Avenue! Surely this was the street the good Mr. Carmichael meant them to take; but, no, it too came to a dead end without revealing a single church of any denomination. By now they were quite baffled and a little weary, but, unwilling to admit defeat, they trudged along Ngong Road until they came to Third Ngong Avenue!

On each of these streets they were rewarded by a profusion of brilliant bougainvillea, jacaranda, frangipani and other vividly flowering trees and shrubs; but, until they reached the very end of Third Ngong Avenue, no Baptist church. There they came upon a small stone building where a middle-aged American couple, obviously dressed for church and looking somewhat anxious, rushed to greet the Grindalls. Mr. Carmichael was embarrassed at having given such imprecise directions.

"Bless you, it could have been worse," he said with a chagrined laugh. "Had you continued, you would have come to Fourth and then Fifth Ngong Avenues!"

After church the party drove through Nairobi's teeming streets to a small cottage on the south edge of the city. Seeing their approach, a tall, elderly man in khaki shorts straightened up from the flower bed in which he was working. At his exuberant hail on recognizing the Carmichaels, a tiny gray-haired woman appeared in the doorway, drying her hands on her apron. Mr. Carmichael made the introductions. The Andersons were delighted to receive visitors "from home." Both were deeply tanned from years under the tropical sun, but there the resemblance ended. Margaret Anderson was a plump little bird, barely five feet tall, who peered up at them through thick lenses that spoke of severely impaired vision. She chattered incessantly in the manner of one who is starved for conversation.

Her husband, a rangy six feet two of lean muscle that belied his seamed features and balding, white-fringed dome, ushered the visitors to lawn chairs under a flowering cape-chestnut tree.

Reluctant to miss a word, but mindful of the demands of hospitality, Margaret broke away and disappeared into the cottage. She emerged a moment later with a tray of glasses and a pitcher of lemonade. Lowrie was already launched upon a discussion of their forty-year ministry in Africa.

Shortly after Lowrie's ordination and marriage, the two had been sent out to that ancient, primitive country formerly called Nubia, now Sudan. There they had labored happily among the people of the Nuer tribe. They raised their family in this place, inaccessible except by air, and refreshed themselves with infrequent vacation trips to their home state of Pennsylvania. The coming of independence brought Sudan only instability and a succession of military dictatorships, each more repressive to its subjects and more hostile to Christianity than its predecessor. Finally, only a few months before the Grindalls arrival, all foreign missionaries were summarily expelled.

Although Lowrie Anderson was only a few years from mandatory retirement at the time of their expulsion, the two doughty old-timers went directly to Nairobi and from there applied for a new mission assignment in Africa. It chanced that the African Church,* headquartered in Nairobi, was at the time looking for trained people to participate in an experimental program called Maasi Rural Development. The work was centered at a mission station called Olooseos, forty-five miles southwest of Nairobi.

Denny, the horticulturalist, listened with growing interest and asked many penetrating questions. Lowrie Anderson responded

---

* A pseudonym

with an invitation. "How would you folks like to drive out to the station with us tomorrow?"

The two tourists accepted with delight. With three free days on their hands before their scheduled homeward voyage, this seemed a perfect conclusion to their African adventure.

The drive to the station in the open Australian vehicle consumed over two hours. After leaving Nairobi the road soon deteriorated into a rutted, stony, twisting track through increasingly wild-looking undeveloped country. After proceeding a few miles they passed through the town of Ngong, a dusty collection of ramshackle houses and commercial buildings of concrete and galvanized iron. Robed people, elaborately adorned with ear ornaments, stared at them. The women were completely bald and wore wide, colorful beaded collars.

"Maasai," said Lowrie. "They're different from any people on earth. From this moment, you will never fail to recognize them."

"Why are their heads and faces red?" asked Jeanne. "And why do the women have no hair?"

"The red is ocher mixed with sheep fat, their favorite cosmetic," Lowrie explained. "The women shave their heads throughout life. The men shave theirs when they enter and leave warriorhood, roughly from age fifteen or sixteen to age thirty or so. Considering the vermin that infest their houses, it's pretty sound hygiene."

Abruptly on leaving the town, they found themselves climbing a long, winding grade that presently opened on a breathtaking sight: the vast, barren windswept Rift Valley. Lowry set the brake and switched off the engine. For a time no one spoke, for words seemed inadequate to express their impressions.

The Great Rift Valley splits the Earth for nearly a quarter of its circumference, from the Jordan River far to the north and to the mouth of the Zambezi in the distant south. From time immemorial it has been forming itself at an infinitely slow rate by the shifting of continental plates, the only such geological process anywhere except on ocean floors. At about one inch a year, approximately the growth rate of a human fingernail, the Rift lives up to its name, widening and deepening inexorably so that one day millennia hence its ends will open upon the Indian Ocean, its floor will flood with seawater and the Horn of Africa will become an island larger than Madagascar, assuming, of course, that neither God nor man intervenes.

Some scientists declare that the Rift is the birthplace of humanity. Not far from this viewpoint is the famed Olduvai Gorge, where Louis and Mary Leakey found ancient bones believed by many to be those of man's earliest ancestors.

Lowrie switched on the ignition and began the long descent down the face of the escarpment. "We'll come back here for another look," he promised. "Right now, there's more we want to show you out at the station."

As they entered upon the valley floor, where scrub growth and scattered trees provided limited cover, they began to see wildlife. Several giraffe ran beside them, their graceful, fluid motions deceptively unhurried. "How fast would you say they're going, Denny?" Lowrie asked.

"Oh, I'd say about eighteen or twenty," Denny answered.

"Take a look at the speedometer," Lowie suggested.

Denny noted that their vehicle was moving at thirty-five miles an hour. But despite the speed, the giraffe were easily keeping pace, seemingly by intent.

"They're so friendly!" Jeanne exclaimed. "They seem quite tame."

"They know they're safe. The Maasai never harm them, nor for that matter, any other wild animals except predators. Maasai giraffe are different from the reticulated giraffe. Those long, beautiful eyelashes are stiff as wire, so their eyes are protected when they browse on thorn trees."

They also saw zebra, a small herd of hartebeest and, in the distance, several skulking spotted hyenas. Presently they passed a clump of green growth in the shade of which a large male lion gnawed with seeming indifference at the red-boned carcass of a wildebeest. Although apparently gorged to acute indigestion, the lion refused to yield the remains of his meal to the vultures that swooped and hopped nearby. From the offensive odor, the travelers realized that the kill was not recent.

The vehicle topped a low-rise opening onto a broad, grassy plain. Lowrie slowed to a stop and pointed. Following his gesture, the visitors saw a compact group of dusky figures moving swiftly about a half mile away.

"Warriors," said Lowrie. "Take a look with the binoculars."

Through the glasses, the troop leaped into startling clarity. Six lithe young men, each garbed in a brief wraparound skirt of earth tone and each carrying a broad-blade spear held vertically, moved in close formation but without apparent effort across the savannah. All wore their hair in braids, heavily ochered and cut square midway between shoulder and waist. They jogged with their heads thrown back and their eyes half closed, apparently taking in nothing around them. Their smoothly muscled legs, ornately decorated with chalk tracings, pumped in time to some silent rhythm.

"They're beautiful, but they look so . . . oblivious," Jeanne commented. "Haven't they seen us?"

"Oh, they've seen us all right," Lowrie chuckled. "That's the moran way of showing utter disdain for everything except their warrior fraternity. Their conceit is quite unbelievable."

"Do all the young men become warriors?" Denny asked.

"They do if their fathers follow tradition. Christian Maasai discourage it. They spend the best fourth of their lives, precious time when they could be preparing for a useful career, plaiting their hair, painting their faces and legs and courting girls who are really children: mere nine- and ten-year olds. 'Courting' is a euphemism, of course; they are not allowed to marry until they graduate into elderhood, but their sexual activity, even from early childhood, is incredible."

Soon after this encounter, the party arrived at a low hilltop, rising modestly above the surrounding valley floor. As the vehicle slowed to a stop, the Grindalls saw many evidences of current activity. Two newly constructed houses, one frame and the other of stone, stood in the midst of a clutter of building materials.

"Welcome to Olooseos," said Lowrie. As the group got out of the car and strolled about the grounds, he recounted the story of how the mission came into being.

"A few years ago, the Maasai were suffering from one of the terrible droughts they experience so often. Many of their animals died, and some of the children too. When the drought became severe, they did what they always do . . . drove their herds into the highlands in search of grass and water. While they were in their temporary camps, a wandering evangelist spoke to them. One of those who heard his message was a powerful chief named ole Moiko. By the way, 'ole' means 'son of.' This chief was so moved by the gospel message that he abandoned his pagan beliefs and accepted Christ on the spot. He's a wonderful fellow; we know him quite well. He has now taken the name of Moses, following the custom of all African converts to Christianity. Well, this ole Moiko, or Moses, continued to ponder what he had learned long after the rains came and the clans returned to their villages. His influence was great, so he assembled all the elders of the seventeen villages in this district, which is known as Olosho-Oibor." Lowrie pronounced this name

"Oley Shaybor."

"I should point out," he continued, "that Maasai chiefs have little or no real authority, and their influence varies according to their personal prestige. Ole Moiko is held in great respect, so his words carry unusual weight. This was a very large council, perhaps as many as two hundred elders representing the seventeen villages. As they squatted on the ground, the chief addressed them along these lines, as I have the story:

Hear my words, Maasai. The Christian God is powerful and compassionate, not aloof like Engai. He sent his son, Jesus, down to earth to feed the hungry and heal sick people of their diseases. This Jesus can even bring dead people back from the long sleep. I am told that his followers belong to a tribe which they call a church. They, too, feed the hungry and treat the sick, though they cannot raise the dead. Maasai, we have suffered much. We must ask this Christian tribe to come here and help us overcome our troubles. If we do not do this, soon we will be no more.

"Ole Moiko's words stirred great debate, for the notion of inviting outsiders onto tribal land was unthinkable to many of the elders. Nevertheless, they recalled all too painfully their recent tribulations, so in the long run his proposal won them over. Being shrewd bargainers, they then took up the question of how to induce these outsiders to come help them. In their culture it's unusual to do anything without compensation. Again, Chief ole Moiko was ready with an answer: 'We will give them The Place of the Black Mud, Olooseos, so they will have water and can build their *engang* near us.'

"This raised another storm of objections. The Maasai were reluctant to give up the good springs that gave this place its name, but eventually ole Moiko won out on this point also. The clan made the offer to the African Church, sponsors of the evangelist who had spoken to them in the highlands, and when the church accepted their offer, the Maasai Rural Development program was born."

"What are the goals of the program?" Denny wanted to know. "We want to develop a model agricultural center complete with all the farming practices that can be readily assimilated by the Maasai people; that is, we plan to introduce the kinds of crops and livestock species that can be expected to do well here and show the most practical methods of cultivation and animal husbandry. The Maasai are intensely curious people, although they are also very resistant to change. We hope their curiosity will overcome their resistance so that they will gradually imitate what they see here and by that means achieve a healthier, more stable way of life."

Margaret broke in to remind her husband that it was time to leave if they were to visit the Maasai village at Kasamis and still have enough daylight to return to Nairobi before dark.

The terrain was extremely rough and the road almost nonexistent as they penetrated deeper into the arid valley. Lowrie showed no concern as he pushed the rugged vehicle into seemingly impenetrable brush and over jagged rocks. Following his advice, the Grindalls clung to their seats to avoid being tossed out. Still they were able to marvel at the changing scenery and the variety of birds and animals they encountered along the way. They passed a herd of eland and a far-off dark, moving mass that Lowrie identified as cape buffalo. As they rounded a turn, a file of impala sprang across the road, forming for an instant a perfect arch of airborne bodies. A lone bustard stalked through the tawny grass in search of snakes or lizards, and soon what seemed to be a distant black stone elevated a long neck and magically became a male ostrich.

In every lone tree a bird of prey perched motionless. Abruptly, an eagle plummeted from one of these and, with an explosion of feathers, veered away with a lark in its talons. Noting the shocked looks on his guests' faces, Lowrie said with a smile, "Life is real, life is earnest, and its goal is not to be somebody's lunch. But sometimes it happens. Out here it doesn't pay to be on the wrong end of the food chain."

As they approached what appeared to be the rim of a bluff that fell away sharply into a shallow basin, Lowrie parked. He informed them that they would cover the rest of the trip on foot. Before leaving the vehicle he kicked thornbrush around the wheels. "Hyenas love to chew tires," he explained. "I'm sure none of us wants to walk to Nairobi."

An indistinct footpath led to the rim of the plateau on which they were located and angled steeply down the rugged slope into the basin below. The going was difficult as the party scrambled down the rocky path. At one of their frequent rest stops, Jeanne asked, panting, "Where is this village you're taking us to?"

With a gesture at the open valley floor below, Lowrie said in mock surprise, "Why, right there in front of you. Don't you see it?"

Following his gesture they saw what appeared to be a collection of earth mounds or boulders in a roughly oval configuration, enclosed by a circle of thornbrush. Otherwise, the landscape stretched away to the horizon, brown and featureless except for scrubby trees and rocks. As they studied the cluster of mounds, they began to observe signs of activity.

Enjoying his guests' astonishment, Lowrie said quietly, "You're looking at the village of Kasamis. Population about fifty souls, more or less. The men are all out with their cattle. The women and kids have already seen us and most of them are hiding."

"Hiding?" Jeanne echoed with a touch of dismay. "If we're frightening them perhaps we shouldn't. . . ."

"It's all right," Lowrie assured her. "They will be disappointed if we don't pay them a visit. Margaret and I have been here several

times, so they know they can trust us. They know we aren't going
to bring anyone they need to fear."

"How do we greet them?" Denny asked.

"The kids will expect you to touch their heads; that's the conventional adult greeting to a child. They will say 'soba,' which means
hello, and we reply with the same word. To the womenfolk we say,
'takuenya.' "

Denny and Jeanne found themselves experiencing a strong sense
of expectancy. Though they were accustomed to exploring remote
and primitive places, they knew this would be far different, more
exotic than anything they had ever seen or were likely to see again.
Their impression was that of being transported back into some
prehistoric epoch.

As they approached the thorn enclosure, children began to appear. Some wore ragged and soiled short togas of charcoal-colored
fabric. Others wore no garment at all, though even the youngest were
adorned with beaded circlets at neck, wrist and ankle. Swarms of
flies clung unnoticed to their dark faces and bodies. Their eyes were
wide with wonder at the sight of the strangers, but they remained
silent except for the conventional "soba." There was something oddly appealing about the unaffected, trusting way they inclined their
bristly heads for the visitors' touch.

Silently, women began to materialize, their eyes averted and their
faces blank except for a slight air of apprehension. Some were in
skirts or capes of animal skins and some wore brightly colored
garments that appeared to be no more than flat pieces of cloth
draped from the shoulders and fastened at their throats. Each wore
a wide collar of varicolored, intricately patterned beads. Their feet,
like those of the children, were bare and smeared with dung. Without exception, their heads were clean-shaven and coated with red
ocher and animal fat.

Lowrie Anderson greeted the village women in Swahili. Some
responded with a mute nod; one older woman replied haltingly in
the same language.

"She confirms what I told you: the men are in the hills with the
cattle, but she bids us welcome and invites us to enter her house."

As they moved about the compound, the Grindalls were overwhelmed by the quantity of animal excrement, through which the
barefoot women and children waded with perfect indifference. The
outer walls of the dwellings, being coated with dung to cement the
mud beneath, were of a faded green or brown color, depending on
how recently the hovel had been constructed or repaired. A stifling
barnyard odor pervaded the area. Noticing his guests' congealed
expressions, Lowrie said apologetically, "Perhaps I should have prepared you for this, but I didn't want to discourage you from coming.
Are you ready to visit this lady's house? I assure you it will be an
experience you won't forget."

Always observant of construction details, Denny noted with interest the perfect arch that crowned the narrow entryway as they
lowered their heads and squeezed through. A mud wall loomed
dimly before them, dictating a turn to right or left. The room to the
left was merely a stall for animals too young to be exposed to the
hazards of the corral at the center of the enclosure, which was
occasionally invaded by predators despite the thornbrush barricade.
Lowrie steered them to the right. At once they were enveloped in
thick darkness that was relieved only by a faint gleam through a
small opening in the low roof. Here the choking barnyard stench
mingled with the acrid smell of wood smoke. In the unventilated
hovel these odors, combined with the oppressive darkness and the
confining stricture of the low ceiling and narrow passages, induced
in the visitors a desire to escape that was close to desperation; yet
their fascination with the place overcame their uneasiness. As their

eyes adjusted to the gloom, various details began to emerge.

The wood smoke, they discovered, came from a fire pit in the center of the earthen floor. In the corners of the room lay some animal skins, which appeared to be the beds of the occupants. A pile of charcoal and some sticks of firewood were along one wall. Two crudely carved stools, a collection of calabashes of various sizes and shapes, some leather pouches and a few bone and wood tools made up the balance of the hut's furnishings.

Lowrie's voice came quietly out of the darkness. "You are looking at a typical Maasai house. Scientists believe the design has not changed in five centuries."

"Why is it so dark?" asked the ever-practical Denny. "It would be easy enough to frame some windows in the walls."

"The darkness is a blessing," Lowrie said. "Flies avoid the light, so the Maasai make their houses as lightproof as possible to escape them. That doesn't mean, though, that the darkness keeps out snakes, lice, fleas, termites and scorpions."

"How horrible!" Jeanne shuddered.

As they started the long drive back to the city, their conversation was subdued as they reflected on what they had seen. Jeanne was first to speak. "Those poor people. I'll never forget their patient, suffering faces. They must have terrible health problems."

"Of course they do," Lowrie sighed. "Where does one begin to describe them? More than half the children die in infancy or soon after. Intestinal and respiratory infections are the major killers of the young. They have all sorts of eye diseases, including an appalling incidence of blindness. Of course, the flies breed by the millions in all the animal feces, then prey on the people. And if it isn't flies, it's the water. The Rift is so dry in most places that they have no springs or year-round streams to speak of, so they have to depend on impounded rainwater. Naturally their herds, as well as all the wild animals, share the water holes with them. When the water starts to evaporate and the animals continue to wade and defecate in it, the smell alone is enough to make one ill.

"Then there are untreated injuries of every kind. Babies and small children often roll into the fire pits in their sleep. Some don't survive; others are maimed for life. Broken bones are seldom properly set, so we get grotesquely deformed limbs. The women suffer from pregnancy-related conditions, and many die in childbirth. Men are sometimes mauled by lions and leopards and a few are gored by buffalo. Diarrhea and dysentery are almost universal. Other conditions that are seldom even heard of in your world—leprosy, tetanus, sleeping sickness, elephantiasis—are common. Because of their diet and lack of dental care, the Maasai have a lot of trouble with their teeth. By the way, did you see how many are missing two lower incisors?"

"I noticed that," said Denny. "Why do so many lose the same two teeth?"

"They don't lose them; their parents extract them when the permanent teeth come in. The practice is so old that no one is even sure why it is done. One legend has it that it's supposed to protect them from starving if they contract tetanus . . . lockjaw. According to this notion, the patient can be fed through the opening in the teeth. I don't vouch for the story, however."

"Are their health problems worse than those of other Africans?" Jeanne wanted to know.

"Probably, for a number of reasons. First, being herdsmen, they live in intimate contact with their animals and, consequently, suffer terribly from the flies that breed in the animal feces. Second, their water, as I mentioned, is not only scarce but bad. Also, they are cut off by their tribal exclusiveness from the health care that is available to other tribes, poor as that care often is. But the worst of their problems is diet. No other people in the world subsist by choice on a diet consisting almost exclusively of cow's blood mixed with milk."

Denny was astounded. "By choice? With so much game available?"

"Amazing, isn't it? You see, their religion forbids them to eat wild animals and teaches them that all birds are an abomination. Oh, they have been known to eat gazelle occasionally, but nothing else."

The sun had plunged below the hills, and shadows were gathering swiftly. Lowrie switched on the headlights. A pair of yellow eyes gleamed by the roadside ahead, "Lioness," said Lowrie. "Her lord and master is waiting in a tree somewhere for her to bring him his dinner."

On Tuesday the Andersons took their guests to the promontory where, two days earlier, the Grindalls had first beheld the Great Rift Valley. The wind that had then threatened to blow them away was now only a gentle breeze stirring the lion grass. Fleecy clouds sailed across a sky of dazzling blue, spreading their shadows like moving stains across the valley floor below. The occasion for this trip was a picnic. As the four found a suitable patch of ground and began settling themselves, they were grateful for the wind's moderation and for the partial cloud cover that gave welcome relief from the sun.

In their brief time together the two couples had formed a bond of friendship that in other circumstances might have taken months to achieve. For three days they had spent nearly all their waking hours together, sharing memories and discovering common interests. Margaret, the talkative one, and Jeanne, the quiet listener, had found an easy harmony together. Lowrie, the scholarly visionary, and Denny, the practical man of action, recognized in each other a shared idealism.

For once, conversation was sparse and the mood of the group subdued. All were aware that the *African Meteor,* now docked at

Mombasa, would sail in less than thirty-six hours, carrying the Grindalls halfway around the world to their Seattle home. Denny and Jeanne absorbed the scene spread before them, storing it for future enjoyment. As Lowrie studied them, a faint smile played across his face.

"Tell me what you see out there, Denny," he suggested softly.

Denny pondered a moment, then answered lightly. "Well, I see a whole lot of sunburned real estate that could sure use a good rain."

"Let me tell you what I see: what's really there but hidden from our eyes. I see tens of thousands of God's people who have been left behind in humanity's rush to conquer this planet. People who may be living out their last days without knowing it."

Denny was impressed by the older man's earnestness but unwilling to accept his prophecy. "Why so, Lowrie? Don't the Maasai have the same opportunities as their neighbors?"

"It's not lack of opportunity that threatens them. It's culture. Their own culture. They cling stubbornly to a way of life that is doomed by the changes that are taking place around them."

"What changes?" asked Denny.

"Oh, the things we like to call progress: new towns, highways, airfields, plantations, resorts, game parks. All that kind of development has jumped ahead with independence, and it's only going to accelerate. The new government is already talking about breaking up these ancient tribal lands into small holdings. When that happens it will deal a death blow to the nomad's way of life."

"Will that necessarily be bad? The whole world is changing, whether we like it or not. It seems to me, the important thing is for people to adjust to the changes."

"I agree, and that's exactly the problem. The Maasai are obliged to change, but they refuse to do so. If they don't adapt, I believe they may not survive as a people. The idea is not new, you know. Back before World War 1 an Englishman wrote a book entitled *The Last of the Maasai*. It turns out his prophecy was premature, but it may not have been incorrect."

"Do the Maasai recognize this danger?" Denny asked.

"A few do. The visionary ones. But there aren't many of those. The powerful voices in their councils usually belong to the reactionaries: the traditionalists." Denny pondered the gloomy words. Problems considered insoluble always bothered him. "Isn't anything being done about it?" he demanded.

"Well, Margaret and I are doing what we can, but our powers are limited and our time is growing short. In a few more years I'll be obliged to retire. The Kenyan federal government is new and inexperienced, and it faces a host of other problems. The initiative will have to come from outside the tribe, for the Maasai simply don't have leaders qualified to do what is needed."

Denny fell silent, thinking about his friend's words. *What a challenge these two have taken on,* he reflected. *What a triumph it will be if somehow they manage to pull it off!*

As if reading Denny's thoughts, Lowrie spoke again, quietly but with great earnestness. "You and Jeanne have no idea how much your visit has meant to us, Denny. We couldn't love you more if we'd known you all our lives. We'd really like to have you come back soon and help us."

In the context of the occasion, Lowrie's suggestion seemed more sentimental than serious: an impulsive outburst inspired by their imminent parting. Denny's arm circled Jeanne's shoulders. "Wouldn't that be great, honey?" he asked.

She smiled and gave his hand an affirming squeeze.

"I'm quite serious, you know," Lowrie said calmly. "Margaret and I have talked it over already. We both believe the four of us could work together in perfect harmony and accomplish great things.

Jeanne has just the right temperament to work with the women; they
would love her, and she could teach them so much! And Denny,
I see that you have already caught this vision of mine. If I searched
the world over, I couldn't find a better partner to make my dream
become a reality. You're a horticulturalist . . . exactly what's needed,
as well as a practical, versatile, energetic man. If the two of you were
to carry on after us, who but God knows what wonderful things
might be done?"

The Grindalls stared at each other, dumbstruck by the audacity
of the plan. Denny groped for a suitable response.

"What can we say? It's a beautiful idea and both of you have
become very special to us. We love Africa, and we've come to love
you. But you know, we still have a lot to do at home. We have a
business to operate, with employees and customers who depend on
us. Our children are grown, but they still need our help. And there
are grandchildren coming along too. You see, we're still a long way
from retirement. You can be sure, though, that we will pray about
it, and if the Lord wants us out here, I know he'll find a way to bring
us back."

Five
WORK TRIP TO KENYA
1970

Back in Seattle, Denny and Jeanne plunged at once into their familiar round of activities. Under the temporary management of their son Paul the nursery and garden store had done well during their absence. Now many of their regular customers came in to learn about their trip, for in those days East Africa was still a remote and little-known place. Their church friends were also keenly interested; soon they were asked to tell their story at a Sunday-evening potluck dinner. Denny edited his slides and put together an entertaining narration. The show was pronounced a hit; moreover, Denny found that he enjoyed the experience, though Jeanne, always a little shy in front of a group, was less enthusiastic.

In the days that followed, despite their many activities, Africa was never far from their thoughts. Often one or the other would say, "I wonder how Margaret and Lowrie are." Curiously, their absorption with these thoughts did not fade over time. The year came and went. Then 1970 arrived, promising to be their best business year ever. One day a strange-looking letter arrived: a pale blue envelope imprinted with the head of an elephant and bearing the stamp of Kenya.

"It's from the Andersons!" Jeanne exclaimed. She read it aloud. Denny listened intently.

The message was brief and direct. Their old friends missed them and wanted to see them again. Great changes were taking place at Olooseos.

If the Grindalls were still unable to take the step that Lowrie had proposed earlier, would they at least come for a long visit, say a three-month working vacation?

Denny's eyes shone as Jeanne finished reading the letter. "What do you say, honey?" he asked eagerly. Her look was answer enough. "Let's do it," he exclaimed, clasping her hand in his. Their decision, they realized, had been made long ago.

The next outgoing mail carried their acceptance. Paul was reinstated as manager of the store. Denny, who had been mentally designing a Kenyan vegetable garden even before the invitation from the Andersons, began filling a small suitcase with promising species of vegetable seeds. They packed mostly working clothes, plus a few dressier garments for special occasions. After booking passage on a French freighter scheduled to sail for Le Havre in July, they made a special midweek visit to their church.

University Presbyterian was at the time undergoing even more than its usual growth and change. Beloved old Dr. Munger had moved on to a faculty post at Fuller Theological Seminary. He had been replaced by the Reverend Richard Langsford, whose principal

associate was O. Vaughan Chamness, Minister for Missions. It was
Chamness whom the Grindalls came to see.

Ordained in 1924 after graduating from San Francisco Theological Seminary, Vaughan Chamness spent the following eighteen
years in Korea. Part of the time he was superintendent of a leper
hospital. The balance of time, he was pastor of countless churches,
never fewer than seven at a time. With the onset of World War 2,
when all foreign Christians were driven out of the Far East, Chamness returned to San Francisco to serve as professor of visual education at his former seminary. Later, from 1962 until his assignment to UPC in 1965, he ran the audiovisual department of the
Synod of Syria and Lebanon in Beirut. His two great occupational
passions were mission service and audiovisual communication.
Now, in the twilight of his long career, Chamness still radiated
youthful energy and enthusiasm. His broad, seamed face, perma-
nently darkened by his years under the sun, glowed with excitement
as he listened to the Grindalls describe their forthcoming adventure.
Lacing his fingers behind his grizzled crewcut, he leaned back in
his chair and beamed.

"God bless both of you. You are exactly the right people to be
doing this. And who but God knows what may come from it? How
I envy you!" He turned quickly to his second interest. "Take lots of
pictures . . . hundreds of 'em. Use slide film; you can always make
prints from them if you want to, and you can share slides with more
people. The light out there is wonderful—brilliant, clear, intense—
so use low-speed film. ASA 50 is fast enough, and it will give better
quality than that high-speed stuff. And be sure to keep a photo
notebook."

"Hold on!" Denny protested. "Are you planning to send us on a
lecture tour?"

"Who knows? Be ready for anything God may call on you to do.

Keep a journal, and record everything that happens." As he saw them out, he added, "I'll pray for you every day, and I'll ask the congregation to do the same. Now, don't forget to send me some postcards."

After a leisurely and relaxing voyage, they spent a few days in Paris, Rome and North Africa. It was early evening of September 2 when they finally arrived at the Nairobi airport. There they met immediate frustrations. When their entry permit did not satisfy the Kenyan immigration official, they fretted at the delay, fearing it would cause them to miss the Andersons. Then when they finally did receive their visas, they were dismayed to discover that the Andersons were not at the airport to meet them. They later learned that their wire from Addis Ababa had gone astray, as do many African telegrams. After three futile hours on the telephone, they gave up and took a cab to the Norfolk Hotel, where they wearily put up for the night.

The next morning their fortunes improved. They managed to contact a senior official of the African Church, who promised to get word to the Andersons that their guests were waiting to be picked up. In the next few hours they enjoyed what was to be their last warm bath for three months, shared lunch on the terrace with some Peace Corps volunteers and reorganized their luggage. In late afternoon a Land Rover drew up before the hotel and an exuberant Lowrie Anderson sprang out to greet them with bear hugs.

They found Olooseos wondrously changed in two years. Where formerly there had been only two partially completed houses plus some tents, temporary shelters and piles of building materials, they now saw an orderly compound with a good barn, tool shed, workshop, chicken yard, bunkhouse and corral. In the corral were some hump-backed cows which, Lowrie explained, were to be crossed with Maasai cattle for greater disease resistance. There was also a sheepfold with a hundred or so Egyptian fat-tailed sheep. Several Maasai workmen lounged near the barn, staring curiously at the newcomers.

Margaret Anderson flew out of the door, shrieking a welcome, as soon as the Land Rover drew up. Behind her came four younger people: the Andersons' daughter Pat, Pat's teen-age son from Long Island, an English youth named Michael McCoy and a Scottish nurse, Mairhi McRitchie.

Margaret had prepared a wonderful dinner. During the meal there was much laughter and sharing of news, with the younger people listening attentively and entering freely into the joyful spirit of the occasion. After the table was cleared, Lowrie convened an evening prayer service, giving thanks to the Creator for bringing dear friends from America and petitioning his favor in the work that lay ahead.

Before retiring, Denny and Jeanne strolled outdoors to experience the African night. Conditioned as they were to ceaseless urban noise, they were awed by the pervasive silence. Overhead the sky was blue-black velvet, studded with stars that faintly illuminated the sharply rising Ngong Hills and the distant Rift escarpment.

Abruptly the stillness was shattered by a tremendous, full-throated roar, sustained and challenging. Although it came from a considerable distance, the swelling sound in that vast ocean of silence made it seem frighteningly close. Then they heard a soft chuckle from the direction of the house. Lowrie's tall figure was framed by lamplight in the doorway.

"Our friend Simba is declaring the boundaries of his territory . . . about ten square miles. He does that to frighten away the hyenas."

The next morning dawned brilliantly clear and fresh after an overnight rain. After breakfast, as the staff assembled for prayer in the tiny school, the Grindalls listened with interest to the medley of languages: English, Swahili and Maa. At the conclusion of the service Lowrie took Denny for a tour of the grounds while Margaret acquainted Jeanne with the household.

"If you have anything that needs ironing, you'd better get it out," said Margaret. "Today is Friday, the only day we have electricity during daylight, and even today the generator is only on from ten till noon."

Jeanne acted on the suggestion, for the Grindalls' few dress clothes were sadly rumpled at the end of their six-week journey. While the two women were working and chatting, three Maasai youths appeared at the open door.

Their togas were smeared with cow dung and their faces and bodies coated with dust. They were shod in flat cowhide sandals, though Jeanne noted that one, who she realized with a start was blind, wore only one. Each lad carried a slender rod about five feet long . . . the inevitable cattle stick.

At Margaret's cheery greeting, the blind boy replied in a harsh, demanding tone.

"He wants to make sure that Michael will keep his promise," Margaret explained. "He goes to the blind school in Nairobi, but his father made him come back to the village to be circumcised. He's been out of school for three months, and Michael promised to take him back on Monday." After reassuring the blind boy, Margaret served sandwiches and tea to the three youths, who squatted on the porch and devoured the food, then wandered off in the direction from which they had come.

Meanwhile, Lowrie showed Denny around the station. Presently they came to the rim of the hill and stood for a moment looking out over the valley spread below. The place to which they had come obviously lay at the outer perimeter of the station compound. Nearby stood a strange-looking, weather-beaten structure half-concealed by weeds and brush. It appeared to be a small, narrow house, and upon approaching it curiously, Denny discovered that it was mounted on wheels.

"That's the mobile bunkhouse that was used by the crew that built our road," Lowrie explained. "When they finished their work, they just abandoned it and went home. I've mentioned it to the road-maintenance boss, but he doesn't seem interested in recovering it."

Closer inspection revealed signs of eccentric construction, slovenly housekeeping and the ravages of neglect. An ill-fitting door, well below standard height, scraped open noisily as the two men entered. A single window, grimy and covered with cobwebs, let in murky light. The only furnishings inside were a double row of narrow bunks, one above the other, extending the twelve-foot length of the little structure. The floor was ankle-deep in litter. "Maybe the owners won't mind," suggested Denny, "if I remodel it a bit so Jeanne and I can live in it."

"It's not very grand," Lowrie protested.

"Just give me a couple of days and you won't recognize it," Denny assured him. "You and Margaret were crowded before we came, so I'm sure you'll be glad to get us out from under your feet."

"Well, if you don't mind tackling it, go ahead. I'm certain no one will object. You'll find tools and materials in the shop."

Denny set to work at once. In short order he cleared away the trash, tore out the bunks, removed the warped and undersized door and reframed its opening to standard size. In the shop he found a surprising wealth of necessities for his project. He was even able to construct a Dutch door. Also, he attached a porch to the end of the building which overlooked the valley. That would be a delightful place, he judged, to sit with Jeanne in the cool of the evening to view the splendors spread before them. He soon added a window screen, shelving, a breadboard, towel racks and other niceties. Then he invited the others for an inspection. He referred to the remodeled dwelling as the "honeymoon cottage" in memory of the first house he had built on the old Denny homestead plot.

"My goodness!" exclaimed Margaret. "I wouldn't have recognized the place. Does he do things like this at home, Jeanne?"

"Oh, yes," said Jeanne with a quiet twinkle. "He's quite handy to have around the house."

Their first Sunday contrasted sharply with their quiet Sundays at home. While they were dressing for church, a young Maasai woman appeared, calling loudly for help from outside the house. She had walked twenty miles during the night with a badly burned infant in her arms. She told them that the child, an eighteen-month-old boy, had been thrown onto a fire by older children. On examination, his burns appeared so severe that it seemed unlikely his hands could be saved. Denny rushed next door to wake Mairhi, the Scottish nurse, who emerged disheveled but not unduly disconcerted to dress the child's terrible burns. Margaret made breakfast for the mother and baby, then proceeded calmly to do the same for her guests.

The worship service was conducted in the tiny station school, with Chief Moses (the previously mentioned Chief ole Moiko) bringing the message. Two of his wives were in attendance. A shy Maasai boy passed his hymnbook to the Grindalls and helped them with hymn selections and Scripture passages in limited but understandable English. He told them his name was David Kisera. Grateful for his help, they resolved to stay in touch with young David.

Next day, with the start of the work week, Lowrie put Denny to work designing and installing a waterline from the pumphouse to the various locations where water would be needed. Jeanne's major assignment was to be in charge of financial accounts and records, and, when needed, to assist Mairhi in the clinic. On this, her first day, the demands of the clinic made bookkeeping irrelevant. Before evening she had registered eighty-seven patients and processed thirty babies. Processing consisted of weighing and recording each infant, dispensing powdered milk, vitamins, cough syrup and salve to the mothers, and turning the more serious cases over to Mairhi. This incredible volume, she learned from the Scottish nurse during a hasty lunch break, was due to a recent outbreak of measles, a disease to which Maasai infants are especially prone. There were also the usual cases of worms, colds, chest infections, burns, cuts and intestinal disorders from unclean feeding formulae.

"The real trick in Africa," Mairhi told her, "is to make it to age five. If they get that far, they've got a bare chance to grow up."

Jeanne was immediately attracted to the matter-of-fact, plain-spoken Mairhi. As the days passed, the nurse's personal story emerged. She came from Edinburgh, where her father operated a car rental business. His contacts with tourists from the United States had given him a poor opinion of Americans. Furthermore, neither of her parents being Christian, Mairhi's father also harbored a jaundiced view of that religion. Having absorbed something of these prejudices, Mairhi found herself at Olooseos in close contact with the two things her opinionated father detested most. Soon she discovered, in the lives of these four mature American Christians, something she had never possessed and sorely needed. In time she became a Christian. Later, when her parents came to visit her, they too developed a warm friendship with the Andersons and the Grindalls. Eventually Mairhi McRitchie came to be almost like a daughter to Denny and Jeanne.

A dramatic event occurred during the Grindalls' first week that left a mission family homeless and threw Olooseos into turmoil for many days.

At a little distance from the Andersons' stone dwelling stood the frame house of the farm manager, Istvan Chakan, and his wife, Julie, and small daughter, Tinde. This family had come to Olooseos in a strange and somewhat inauspicious way: through the abrupt departure of Chakan's predecessor, Neill Watson.

Watson, although conscientious and hard-working, was not always careful in speech. One day he let slip a racially offensive remark in the hearing of Jerusha, a Maasai nurse. She reported the remark to the African Church authorities, who promptly dismissed Watson and initiated a search for his replacement.

Istvan Chakan was a Hungarian, an ordained Presbyterian pastor and a self-proclaimed "agriculturalist." He had advertised his availability for mission service in an international publication and was engaged without interview, for the church considered his credentials ideal for its needs. He was a strange man: harsh, awkward, proud, touchy and eccentric. His wife bore a look and manner of perpetual injury, and the child, Tinde, was nervous, fearful and unmanageable. Although the Olooseos staff, a close-knit, harmonious group, put itself out to include the Chakans in social activities, the lonely little family usually kept apart.

Soon after taking the job, Istvan began eliminating all traces of his predecessor's work and to install procedures of his own peculiar design. This puzzled the Maasai work crew and disturbed the station director, Lowrie Anderson. First, there was the matter of milk production, which began to drop off alarmingly soon after Chakan's arrival. Upon investigation Lowrie discovered that the cows were being milked only on alternate days on the theory that this would somehow increase their total yield. Lowrie summarily canceled the experiment and put milking back on a daily schedule.

Some time after that Denny noticed that the rams in the flock of fat-tailed were all sporting crimson swatches on their woolly rumps. Inquiry revealed that Istvan, who felt that the Maasai workers would not otherwise be able to distinguish sexes, had marked all the rams.

On another occasion Denny, while visiting several Maasai villages, noticed that each hut had a length of stovepipe projecting from its mud roof. Suspecting this to be another of Istvan's unusual experiments, Denny learned that the farm manager had indeed installed the stovepipes, thinking thereby to eliminate, or at least reduce, the unhealthy smoke inside the hovels. Unfortunately, this innovation did nothing to improve either the ventilation or the appearance of the houses.

But, back to the incident at hand. On a fine Tuesday morning, the Grindalls' fifth day as volunteers, nine members of the Olooseos staff climbed into the Land Rover for a day of shopping and other business in Nairobi. Denny and Lowrie planned to confer with an architect about the design of the proposed church, then pick up some hardware. Margaret and Jeanne would buy groceries for the coming week. The Chakans needed furnishings for their house, and the Andersons' daughter, Pat, and Pat's son, Bob, simply went along for the outing.

In the late afternoon the party regrouped at a designated place for the return trip. Lowry suggested that Denny drive in order to get accustomed to the roads. As the Land Rover angled down the face of the escarpment, a dust column appeared, approaching rapidly from the direction of the station. It could only be the Volkswagen combi racing toward them from Olooseos, and its speed portended an emergency.

The combi soon burst into view, weaving erratically, and skidded to a stop. White-haired old Joram tumbled out of the car and staggered toward them, eyes rolling and tears streaming down his dark face.

"Room burn down! Room burn down!"

Only then did they see the pillar of smoke that was rising from the direction of the station.

Lowrie relieved Joram at the wheel of the combi and led the other vehicle at breakneck speed over the few remaining miles. The two cars arrived just in time to see the roof of the Chakan house collapse in an inferno of flame and sparks. Mairhi, Michael and the Maasai crew stood watching helplessly.

The Chakans, now having only the clothes on their backs, were beside themselves. After the other staff members tried without success to comfort them, Lowrie and Mairhi drove them all the way back to Limuru, a suburb of Nairobi, where some Hungarian friends, stupefied by the news, took them into their home.

As muffled explosions from the embers rumbled throughout the evening, a wonderful thing happened, though. Chief Moses convened a meeting of Maasai elders under a thorn tree near the construction site of the church. Having seen smoke from their distant villages, about eighty men gathered at Olooseos, and under Chief Moses' leadership they conferred at length in agreement with tribal custom following any unusual event. The next morning the chief informed Margaret that he had obtained some blankets for the stricken family. Such gestures are unusual among unconverted Maasai.

An insurance adjustor drove out from Nairobi to investigate the fire. From him the staff learned what had happened. An electric heater in Tinde's bedroom had been left switched on. This invitation to disaster had gone unnoticed because the electricity from the station generator operated only between 6:00 and 10:00 each evening. Foolishly, the Chakans had allowed the generator schedule to serve as an automatic control on the heater in the child's bedroom. The twisted metal heater was found beside the charred remains of Tinde's bed and too near the window curtain, the investigator concluded. When the generator came on during the family's absence, conditions were ideal for a conflagration. Only when all the lights on the station abruptly went out did those remaining at Olooseos become aware of the tragedy; when Michael went out to investigate, the fire was already out of control.

On Thursday the Andersons drove to the airport with their daughter and grandson, who were returning to their Long Island home. Mairhi and Michael went along to buy medical supplies. In their absence, Jeanne was in sole charge of the clinic when a Kikuyu woman appeared with her ailing baby girl, whom Jeanne had treated only the day before. She was horrified to discover that the child had lost nine ounces overnight and weighed barely more than five pounds. The poor little thing, a listless bundle of skin and bones, could barely swallow the medicine that Jeanne held to her withered lips. With difficulty, Jeanne made out from the mother that she had not mixed the child's feeding formula with boiling water, as she had been instructed to do. Instead she had used raw cow's milk, which brought on a fearful bout of diarrhea.

The next day, while Denny and Michael were delivering estimates of the fire's damage to the African Church office and Margaret was trying to get the American consul to help evacuate another daughter, Ruth, and her children from war-threatened Aman, Jeanne again worked in the clinic. An old man shuffled in, his eyes reddened and glazed with shock and his white hair matted with blood. As Jeanne cleaned and bandaged the man's head, she contemplated her own growing detachment in the face of the suffering that seemed so commonplace in this afflicted land. Then, when the Kikuyu woman returned with her ailing baby, Jeanne discovered to her satisfaction that the little one had regained six ounces and her bowels had stopped flowing. Gently, Jeanne fed her more milk.

Denny and Jeanne never tired of the view from the porch of the "honeymoon cottage." On clear evenings, just before the great red sun began to vanish behind the western hills, a beautiful transformation occurred. Commonplace objects, when outlined by the fading light, took on a dramatic appearance that was not evident in full daylight. An acacia that moments before had been a perfectly ordinary tree suddenly became a looming silhouette. A Maasai herdsman, standing cross-legged and inconspicuous in the full glare of afternoon, cast a gigantic shadow across the plain. The departing sun's nimbus transformed his ragged toga and cattle stick into a prophet's robe and staff. The dust cloud above a homebound cattle herd became a fiery nebula. Then, when the shadows dissolved and darkness quickly enveloped the landscape, the sky took on a luminous glow that lasted for nearly an hour. Watching in awe, Denny and Jeanne remembered Vaughan Chamness's words about the wonderful quality of African light. They decided the unique phenomenon must be due in part to the absence of air pollution, but even such a sensible explanation could not rob the moment of its magic.

Twilight was a brief intermission in the drama, a silent time of changing light during which the stage was rearranged and a waiting cast of nocturnal players crept from the wings. Then the unseen voices of the night began to speak. A low, arresting cough, like a distant saw cutting hardwood, was the call of a leopard to its mate. A plaintive, high-pitched cry of terror was a cheetah kit summoning its mother when an enemy prowled near. A burst of spine-tingling, demented, barking laughter meant that a hyena pack had picked up the scent of a strayed calf or goat. Seldom, though, did they again hear the mighty roar of a male lion warning intruders away from his domain. Reluctant to abandon such a splendid show but mindful of tomorrow's demands, Denny and Jeanne bid each other good night and retired.

About a week after their arrival Lowrie asked them to help present a film showing at a nearby village. The party of four left late that afternoon in the Volkswagen van. The village was in the valley of Olosho-Oibor, where Lowrie was especially desirous of establishing good relations, for this was to be the starting locale for the Maasai Rural Development experiment.

About fifty men, women and children awaited their arrival. They watched with interest as Lowrie and Denny fastened the screen, a plain white sheet, to the wall of one of the houses, placed the projector on a wooden box and started the portable generator. Lowrie narrated the film in Swahili as the audience crouched in a semicircle, oblivious to the wind that swirled a mixture of red dust and powdered dung about them. Cattle wandered unnoticed through the compound.

The film was a Billy Graham production with a direct and powerful story: the life of Jesus. The audience watched silently, but when the film ended the men promptly launched into their usual lively discussion.

Pleased with the audience's response, Lowrie nevertheless refrained from entering in except to answer questions. "They will talk about this for weeks," he predicted as the party began loading equipment back in the van. "They love all forms of drama: stories, pictures, poetry. The Maasai are fine poets and storytellers themselves."

When the four visitors climbed into the van and settled themselves for the return trip, they were shocked to discover that the Volkswagen's headlights would not come on. On this moonless night, the tracks of the road, which were only faintly visible in daylight, simply vanished. The villagers watched silently as Lowrie fiddled with the switches in mounting frustration. Nothing happened as we tried one switch after another.

"What do we do now, Lord?" he demanded in exasperation. "It has to be a blown fuse," Denny offered. "Do you have any spares?"

After rummaging in the glove compartment, Lowrie shook his head.

Recollections of similar problems with his old Model T Ford flashed through Denny's mind. "How about chewing gum?" he asked. No one came up with any gum.

"Nothing here but some empty wrappers," Lowrie reported.

"That's what I want!" Denny exclaimed. Without offering any explanation, he took one of the gum wrappers Lowrie handed him and, after stripping away the paper, folded the remaining foil in a thin strip. This he inserted into the fuse clamp. "Now try your lights," he suggested.

Immediately, twin beams speared the gloom. The party broke into a cheer as the villagers clapped their hands and howled with de-light. As the van bounced over the rocks and wound around hairpin turns, Denny explained how he had known what to do. "Everyone should have a Model T Ford in his background," he chuckled. "There's no better training for these little emergencies."

Denny was eager to start his garden, for he was hoping to pro-duce mature vegetables before the end of their stay. Lowrie suggest-ed that the shamba be located near the village where the film was shown. The people there were already accustomed to the occasional presence of Whites. Their chief, a man named Mboya, demonstrat-ed unusual openness and cooperation. Although there was no water at the village for irrigation, recent rains had been plentiful, and Denny counted on their continued abundance. With his chemical testing set he determined that the soil was suitable for vegetable growth except for a slight deficiency in potash, which could easily be supplemented.

"What are you going to do about fertilizer?" Jeanne asked.

Denny shrugged. "The elephants have taken care of that for a few thousand years, and the Maasai cattle are doing fine now."

As he discussed the project with Lowrie, Denny continued to worry about water. "Where do the village people get their domestic water?" he asked.

Lowrie pointed to a patch of green high on the Ngong Hills about two miles away. "There are some springs up there where the men water and graze their livestock. During dry periods, when the potholes dry up, the women go up there and scoop what water they can from the springs."

"Let's hike up and take a look," Denny suggested.

The path up the hill was rocky, steep and covered with dense brush that drew blood on the slightest contact. Denny examined the needle-sharp three-inch thorns with amazement. "You've discovered what the Maasai call the *dashopenyo*," Lowrie chuckled. "It means 'wait-a-bit bush.' I think you just found out why."

What they found when they arrived at the green patch on the hillside was not encouraging. Grass grew thick and green in a pleasant swale about an acre in size, but the only visible water was that which had collected in the hoofprints of cattle. Gloomily, Denny concluded that vegetables in quantity would never be grown in the valley of Olosho-Oibor.

Shaking off his disappointment, he plunged with his usual energy into the clearing of a sizeable plot a hundred yards or so from the village. The work was heavy and the sun hot, but he was rewarded by many glimpses of village life. The men watched but offered no aid. Children edged close and giggled shyly when he waved or winked. The women maintained a discreet distance, but sometimes he caught them watching curiously.

One of the men, a strapping fellow in early middle age, showed more interest than the others in the shamba. He always responded with a smile and a friendly "soba" to Denny's greetings. One day as Denny tugged at a stubborn root, the big man laid hold of it with him, and together they drew the root easily from the hard ground.

"*Ashin oleng,*" Denny thanked him, extending his hand. The black hand was surprisingly soft and slender. Pointing to himself, Denny spoke his own name. The Maasai smiled uncertainly. Again Denny pointed to himself and gave his name, then pointed at the other with a question on his face. White teeth gleamed in a smile of comprehension; the big man tapped his chest and said, "Jonah."

Each day Jonah appeared, and with his help, Denny's progress accelerated. Still the other men of the village remained aloof, watching but offering no assistance.

As he studied the daily activities of the villagers, Denny observed how vital rain was to their way of life. The small reservoirs they scooped out with their crude digging sticks and augmented with dams of mud and dung filled quickly during the heavy rains. First of all when the women came with their calabashes to collect water, they sprinkled milk on the surface of the pond. This expressed their thanks to Engai. Then they appealed to him to preserve the precious supply. In spite of these petitions, the waterholes soon began to dry up. Even while water remained, goats, sheep and cattle waded and drank, their hooves breaking down the dams. The filth expelled by the animals, coupled with rapid evaporation, so polluted the water that the women had to sweep away a thick green scum before filling their vessels. Denny concluded that the health problems of the Maasai would never be relieved while these practices continued. They must be able to depend on a constant abundance of pure water; yet how such a miracle was to be achieved continued to baffle him.

When he was not working on the garden, Denny was in Olooseos, finishing the station waterline. One day he noticed a new face among the Maasai workers and hangers-on lounging near the cattle barn. The newcomer was a Black man, apparently a Maasai, for he

spoke Maa fluently and was clearly well known by the regulars. Yet
he was so different in appearance from the others. Instead of cowhide sandals and a dung-smeared toga, he wore street shoes, trou-
sers and a white shirt open at the throat. He was somewhat shorter
and stockier than the other men. His most striking physical feature
was his head. It was bald except for a thick fringe of curly hair
which was rounded impressively, like the dome of a Black Socrates.
Intrigued, Denny asked Lowrie about the stranger.

"Oh, that's Samuel Pulei," said Lowrie. "His Maasai name is Ntienput, but he hasn't called himself that since he became a Christian.
He's a wonderful fellow . . . the only educated Maasai I know. He's
an ordained pastor, now serving a parish at Moranga. He owns a
small house near here—you've seen it about a mile down the road—
where his family lives. He comes to visit them on his days off but
usually spends most of his free time evangelizing. He has an extraordinary spirit and a driving passion to help his people."

"Does he speak English?" Denny asked.

"Yes, quite well. As a matter of fact, he's being sent to England
soon for some special instruction."

Thereafter, Denny took pains to greet the Maasai pastor when
their paths crossed. Samuel Pulei's responses were friendly, though
slightly reserved; however, their separate activities precluded more
than a few brief exchanges.

Six
TEACHING NEW WAYS
TO SURVIVE
1970

As the days passed, each filled with new activities and challenges, Denny began planning a bold new step. One day he went with Jonah to the hillside not far from the springs he had explored with Lowrie. On that previous occasion he had noticed a small gully carved by rains that seemed suitable for the purpose he now had in mind. With Jonah's help, he sealed the gully with a dam of earth and rock to create a small basin. Next he drove the truck to Nairobi and purchased a 500-gallon tank. He positioned the tank downhill from the dam. Then he connected dam and tank with a length of plastic pipe. After fitting a shorter length of pipe on the opposite side of the tank, he and Jonah scooped out a trough below it.

They did not have to wait long. A generous rainfall quickly filled the reservoir, then the filtration tank and finally, from the overflow pipe, the trough below. The builders surveyed their work with satisfaction. The villagers, who had followed these strange activities with mounting interest, lost no time making use of the new water source. The women were delighted to be able to fill their vessels with clean water from the overflow pipe rather than having to dip from a foul, scum-covered water hole. The men noted with approval that their animals drank from the trough, for the steep walls of the gully made the reservoir itself inaccessible.

"You've caught their interest," Lowrie exulted. "They think you're a wizard."

Denny admitted that this had been his objective. The small dam was only an experiment of limited practical value. He had in mind a much more ambitious project that would do some real good but would call for some sacrifices by the villagers.

"I want to involve these men in something that will really help them, but they'll have to work and help pay for it," Denny said.

Lowrie was dubious. "Maasai men don't like to work; they consider it demeaning. As for financing, their only wealth is in their cattle, which they refuse to sell."

Denny held firm. He recognized the difficulties, but he still wanted a chance to sell his idea to the tribesmen. Lowrie agreed to assemble the elders after the church service the following day, Sunday, and to arrange for young David to act as interpreter.

The elders squatted under the spreading branches of a large thorn tree, their arms encircling their knees and their faces impassive. Denny realized that a strong performance would be necessary, for the communication barrier was formidable. He knew only a few words of Maa, and young David Kisera's command of English was not much better. He decided to rely on body language and strong vocal inflections.

He spoke of the sufferings of the Maasai people due to the uncertainty and impurity of their water. Even their animals were unhealthy from drinking bad water; how much more so their children, their wives and themselves. And how quickly the water, bad as it was, disappeared altogether when the rains did not come.

"*Kitioling maisidi* (small water hole) not good," he exclaimed disdainfully as he pointed to an imaginary pool of insignificant size. "*Salangi sabok sedah* (large pond good). Not dirty. Last long time." While saying this, he walked in a circle some twenty yards in diameter, gesturing dramatically to emphasize its abundance. His hearers showed obvious interest, even amazement at this comparison. It was time to drive home his message. Drawing closer, he spoke with great earnestness. He told them that he could help them make such a salangi sabok, one that would provide water even when the rains did not come, but only if they were willing to work hard and spend some money to possess this marvel.

Vociferous discussion broke out among the elders. Young David was hard put to relay all the comments and questions. Where was there such a wondrous source? Why did they not know of it? How can one produce water without rain? How did he propose to capture it? We don't know this stranger. How do we know we will get anything back if we sell our cattle? Denny pointed to the distant patch of green on the hillside where he and Lowrie had investigated. There were springs there, several of them.

By scooping out a good-sized hollow, they would cause the springs to flow more freely. Then they would build a dam, a larger, stronger one than the one he and Jonah had built. This one would withstand storms and the hooves of animals, ensuring that water would always be there for their use.

The elders discussed the proposal vigorously among themselves. The debate was spirited but orderly, with each speaker permitted to have his say. One who resisted the plan and would remain stubbornly opposed to it thereafter was Lakuka, a wealthy elder with several wives and many cattle. He spoke loudly in a harsh voice, walking back and forth and stabbing the ground with his cattle stick for emphasis.

"This foreigner's words sound good, but if we do what he says, it will mean the end of our way of life. His salangi sabok is only the first of many dangerous new ideas he will bring. If we allow him to gain power, he will turn the heads of our women and children. Soon we will be like old bulls that the cows reject."

The elders listened gravely. Some nodded and murmured assent to Lakuka's words. Denny sensed the balance of opinion shifting against him. Then Lainkini, a lean and wrinkled older man, rose stiffly and spoke.

"Maasai, we have seen what this stranger has done among us. He has shown that his heart is warm toward us. Already our cows give more milk because of him. I think we should trust him and try this plan."

Lainkini's endorsement swung the majority to Denny's position, but many were still loud in opposition. Then one of the proponents warned that those who refused to work and sell cattle should get no water when the salangi was completed. These words had a chilling effect on the opposition.

"Most of them like your scheme," said Lowrie, "but that may not mean anything. If you ask them when they want to do it, they will say 'next year' or 'two years from now.' As long as it's in the distant future, they can feel good about it without actually having to do anything."

Denny accepted this as a challenge. "Maasai," he said, "when shall we start to work?"

There was more lively discussion, then one man spoke the consensus. "They say," reported David, "they will start tomorrow morning."

An hour after sunup next day Denny and Lowrie arrived at the village. Some of the women were already going about their chores, but no men were in sight.

"I warned you of this," said Lowrie. "They've already forgotten about it. They're out with their cattle." Nevertheless, he spoke to one of the women in Swahili. When she answered, Lowrie turned to Denny with a look of wonder.

"She says they are up on the hillside waiting for you. They are ready to go to work."

This response exceeded Denny's wildest expectations. Waiting for him by the hillside springs were thirty-two Black men from a primitive culture. He could only communicate with these men with gestures and through the limited linguistic resources of a Maasai youth. They were disposed by long tradition to despise labor; they knew nothing of tools and possessed none. Most had never even seen a concrete structure, much less built one. But they were waiting for him and ready to go to work!

Denny hastily rounded up all the shovels and picks that could be borrowed from the mission and began conducting on-the-job training. He found it difficult at first to keep from laughing at the antics of the tribesmen as they grappled with these strange devices. Then he discovered that restraint was unnecessary. Every Maasai, he found, loves a joke, whether on himself or on another. Denny quickly took advantage of this. First, he demonstrated the technique himself, then passed the tool to the nearest man. If the apprentice did well, he got an approving pat on the back; otherwise, as was more often the case, Denny gave him a pitying look and called him a Durobo, referring to a forest tribe scorned by the Maasai as *pesha* (worthless). This always produced a howl of mirth from the entire crew, including the victim.

These same Maasai, the men of Denny's original work party, bestowed on him that very day a nickname that has stayed with him through the years. As the equatorial sun rose and the temperature with it, he shed his shirt, as was his custom when doing physical labor on a warm day. At the sight of his bare torso the Maasai were utterly dumbfounded. Never had they beheld such a strange-looking human being, for the Maasai, a Nilotic people, have no body hair. The hirsute endowments of Denny Grindall were exactly the opposite. The sandy hair that distinguished him in his youth was rapidly vanishing. The rest of his compact body was densely covered with thick, reddish hair down to the knuckles of his calloused hands. Dropping their tools, the men closed around him to examine the amazing growth of hair. With howls of mirth, they fingered the tawny hairs on his chest and shoulders. Then one of the men pointed at him and exclaimed, "Simba!" The others roared their agreement and repeated the Swahili word for *lion* delightedly. Denny still cherishes his Maasai nickname.

The men were also interested in the baseball cap that Denny wore to protect his balding scalp from the hot sun. He remembered this on his next shopping trip to Nairobi where he found similar caps in a sporting goods store. He bought thirty-two caps and distributed them to his crew. The men wore their new caps with pride, not only on the job but also at tribal gatherings to distinguish themselves from those who still refused to support the dam project. This distinction obliged some of the holdouts to change their minds and join the work force. Almost by chance, Denny was becoming an effective motivator.

Before buying materials for the construction of the concrete dam, Denny made sure that the men followed through on their promises to sell cattle to finance the work. By common consent, it was left to each man to contribute according to his ability. The cattle were then driven to a designated rendezvous point where buyers came and placed their bids. Two trusted men, chosen as treasurers by their fellows, collected the proceeds from each sale. Although the cattle sale was successful, Denny knew it would not fully cover the cost of the project. He quietly put up the difference out of his own pocket. He was firmly committed to the ideal of self-help, but he would not allow the project to be jeopardized.

The cattle sale drew considerable local notice, for the Maasai, despite their aloof nature, cannot avoid attracting attention. John Keene, a government official, shook his head in wonder and told Denny, "You are the first person who has ever persuaded any of the Maasai to sell their cattle. I don't know how you did it." The interest generated by the cattle sale naturally focused awareness on the dam project itself and on its builder. Unwittingly, Denny was becoming a public figure.

Each new phase of the job required an elaborate training program. Denny, to whom tools were like extensions of his own hands, soon realized that these men, living only forty-five miles from one of the most modern cities in Africa, were, as Lowrie often said, living like people in the Stone Age.

The thought of it never ceased to fill him with wonder. With patience and humor, he taught them how to use hammer, pliers, nail puller, saw and pickmattock. Watching Denny and laughing at their own mistakes, the men were apt pupils. The wooden structure began to take shape.

There were, of course, some injuries—blisters, smashed thumbs, saw cuts and the like—and for these, Denny was prepared. He kept on hand a simple first-aid kit of bandages, alcohol, iodine and antibiotics, which proved a source of great satisfaction to his crew. A special place in his medicine kit was reserved for a remarkable medication that may be unfamiliar to some of the readers of this book.

During Denny's business years, before the feed and seed store evolved into the garden store and nursery, many of his customers were farmers or dairymen. A product much in demand by these customers came in a square, dark-green tin embellished with a clover-leaf design and labeled "Bag Balm."

Dairy cows, although phlegmatic and unintelligent, are nevertheless stubbornly opinionated creatures. Often, in their efforts to reach grass they are sure is sweeter on the other side of a barbed-wire fence, they disregard their own safety. This tendency has led to countless lacerated udders and has created a brisk demand for Bag Balm.

After hearing his customers describe the wonderful healing properties of this product, Denny began to wonder whether it would do as much for a human as for a cow. Using himself as a guinea pig after receiving a laceration, he discovered that it would! To this day, his medicine chest is never without the square green can with the clover-leaf design, and he made sure to take plenty with him to Africa.

Soon he began to know the members of his crew by name; then slowly they began to emerge as distinct personalities. Jonah, the first Maasai to extend his friendship, remained a favorite. Dignified old Lainkini, scarred, wrinkled and stiff in the joints, was nevertheless eager to pull his share of the load. Young David, though only a boy, was a faithful guide and indispensable as an interpreter. Chief Mboya was the only man among them with real vision. His inquiring mind readily grasped the purpose behind Denny's schemes. Accordingly, Denny learned to introduce each idea to the chief and let Mboya sell it to the others. A fine esprit began to develop. Individually, the men were very competitive, but they worked well together. There was an air of excitement about the project, for all had been caught up in the spirit of accomplishment. Denny, noting this, made certain to turn each task into a contest.

After pouring concrete into wooden forms, Denny and "the fellows," as he referred to his crew, cleared a swath through the brushy hillside and flatland from the dam to the village. Then they laid plastic pipe down its course. The work was hot, dusty and backbreaking, so by the time the concrete was cured, the crew rejoiced to turn to the easier task of stripping forms. Everyone was eager to see the result of this undertaking, including Maasai from distant clans.

Water from the springs began filling the reservoir even without benefit of rains, an astonishing sight to the Maasai. On November 10, Denny ceremoniously opened a faucet near the little garden and invited the villagers to view the result—little more than a trickle to be sure, but to people who had never seen water flowing from a pipe, a miracle. The women's usual shyness was replaced by shrieks of laughter as they lined up to fill their cans.

Once the domestic demand was satisfied, Denny assigned volunteers to water the vegetable plants in his shamba, using two-gallon sprinkling cans he had bought in Nairobi. This too became a game. The Maasai, who for centuries had looked down on farmers, took personal interest in each plant as they watched it grow.

Denny's predictions about the soil fertility and beneficial climate were soon confirmed. Never had he seen such splendid potatoes, such long and succulent carrots, such leafy lettuce and such green and tender spinach! And as a special blessing, his little patch at first attracted no enemies. For a time, no eland, impala or burrowing parasites discovered the new garden.

The villagers observed the growing vegetables with interest but showed no inclination to eat them. Denny and Jeanne showed their own enthusiasm, then begged the people to try a taste. The Grin-dalls, of course, understood the ancient taboos that caused the evident reluctance. Jonah was the first to try a carrot. After an apprehensive bite, while the others watched anxiously, he grinned with delight, finished the carrot and held out his hand for more. Others followed suit, and soon all the carrots were gone. Denny offered the tops to a nearby goat and was rewarded with a grateful bleat as the green morsels vanished. The villagers broke up with laughter.

Denny was at pains to encourage active participation by any of the men who might show interest in gardening, in the hope that others might be moved by example. He singled out a tall, handsome man named Babai who seemed to be something of a leader and, through David, urged this man to let Denny help him start his own shamba. Babai consented, and the two of them spent the next two days clearing a sixty-by-hundred-foot plot of grass and stones. On the third day, when the planting was to begin, Babai's two wives came in his place, explaining that their husband wanted them to raise his food.

Bitterly disappointed by Babai's seeming irresponsibility and laziness, Denny vented his feelings that evening to Lowrie, who heard him through without comment. When Denny paused for breath, Lowrie said with a smile, "Babai is assured by centuries of tradition that his way is the right way. Besides, he knows that if he continues to do 'women's work,' the other men will ridicule him. You don't really think you can overcome that conditioning in three days, do you?"

But Denny was in no mood for rational explanations. Brushing aside Lowrie's words, he fumed, "And another thing, don't these people ever say 'thank you'? Babai acted as though he was doing *me* a favor instead of the other way around! And he's not alone. I've not heard any of them utter a word of thanks since we got here!"

Lowrie regarded him quizzically. "Is that why you're working so hard? To earn their thanks?"

Taken aback, Denny muttered, "No, I suppose not. It's just that I assumed there would be some acknowledgement that they appreciate what we're doing. It seems like only common courtesy."

"The Maasai don't have a word for thanks," Lowrie responded, "although once in a great while you may hear one of them use the Swahili phrase *asanti sana*, 'thank you very much.' "

He paused reflectively, then continued. "Maybe they understand better than we do the words of Jesus: 'It is better to give than to receive,' even though most of them are not Christians. I daresay, they may even consider that returning thanks for a gift or favor might take away some of the blessing that giving bestows on the giver."

Aware that the end of their three-month stay was approaching, Denny stepped up the tempo of his labors. He set to work building a waterhouse, using the high, conical thatched-roof design of the Kikuyu instead of the loaf-shaped mud hut of Maasai design. He and his crew installed showers, sinks, hoses and faucets. Jeanne recorded that the men were soon "sawing and hammering away like mad." The waterhouse became the center of the women's social and domestic activity.

When the waterhouse was completed, Jeanne conducted a simple demonstration to introduce the women to the wonders of doing laundry. She took a shuka from one of them and washed it in a strong solution of powdered soap and water. After rinsing it, she held it up for the women to see. They were astonished at its restored color and even more by the dirtiness of the wash water. Jeanne later bought a twenty-pound box of soap powder and sixty-six wash cloths in Nairobi. She divided the soap powder into sixty-six small plastic bags, one for each of the women who had attended the demonstration, and presented these to her pupils.

Istvan, the farm manager, began complaining loudly that the Grindalls' frequent use of the mission vehicles left him without transportation. Embarrassed and not wishing to cause friction, Denny and Jeanne made plans to rent a car for their own use. When Lowrie learned of the matter, he gave Istvan a royal bawling out for raising such a fuss. The uproar caused the Grindalls to abandon the rental idea and limit their driving, which of course curtailed their activities sharply.

While Denny divided his time between Olooseos and Olosho-Oibor, installing the water system and planting gum trees at the mission and seeding his newly cleared land near the village, Jeanne was struggling with the intricacies of Lowrie's accounting system and dispensing medical help to an ever-growing clientele. The bookkeeping task seemed hopeless. Every time the workers were paid or someone drew cash to purchase supplies in Nairobi, the accounts refused to balance, despite the many frustrating hours Jeanne spent wrestling with bills, scribbled notes and ledger entries.

In the clinic things went better. Jeanne's assurance grew as she gained experience, although some of the cases appalled her, and the work drained her physical and emotional reserves. Treating children was the hardest, for there was an endless series of emergencies. Each successful treatment seemed, at best, to be temporary; there was usually little prospect of correcting the basic problem or preventing complications. The frail little bodies continued to waste away. The burns and cuts, when dressed and bandaged, became reinfected within a day. Mairhi's instructions to the mothers brought only listless nods, promising small chance they would be carried out.

The work in the clinic took its toll on Jeanne's own health, which had never been robust. Colds, influenza and periodic bouts of diarrhea sapped her energy, and physical exhaustion became chronic. Denny, too, was worn out much of the time from his many activities. Their peaceful evenings on the porch of the honeymoon cottage became shorter as, with increasing frequency, they tumbled gratefully into bed as soon as the dinner dishes were cleared and washed.

Monday, October 5, was a day of bedlam at the mission clinic. Fifty or so anxious mothers with sick babies in their arms awaited treatment. Another measles epidemic had broken out. Then toward noon a fearful cry of anguish came from the workers' quarters. A messenger brought word that the wife and month-old baby of one of the workers were dead. The mother, an epileptic, had suffered a seizure and had fallen into the fire pit with the infant in her arms.

Two days later a sick infant died. The baby had contracted measles and thrush at a Nairobi hospital after being treated there for croup. The mother, who was living with her children on land owned by old Joram, wanted to bury the baby near her hut, but Joram would not hear of it; he was terrified by the ancient Maasai belief that the presence of a corpse puts a curse on the nearby living. With difficulty, the staff made other burial arrangements.

One day in late October, a caravan of twenty Land Rovers packed with government officials came to inspect the shamba, the dam project and the mission station. Chief Moses ole Moiko made a long, impressive speech, then dragged Denny up before the group, insisting that he also favor the distinguished visitors with a few words. Jeanne recorded in her diary that when the procession rolled into Olooseos it "looked like a full-scale invasion."

Despairing of ever getting her books to balance, Jeanne instituted a petty cash system with two hundred shillings in coins and small bills in a separate metal box. With this, she noted wistfully, she could at least "hope to keep things straighter."

A little boy arrived at the clinic near death from vomiting, diar-rhea and a urinary infection so severe that he was urinating blood. His parents, desperately poor, knew that he should go to the hos-pital, but they couldn't afford to send him there. Jeanne remembered fifty-three dollars that some friends had given her for charitable use. She gave the money to Mairhi to pay for the boy's hospitalization.

Monday, November 16, was "an unusually wild day," Jeanne not-ed. In pouring rain Mairhri rushed a gravely sick child to the Hikuyu Hospital. Then a lorry arrived with a badly injured young Maasai who had fallen from a tree when the honeybees whose hive he was robbing descended on him in an angry swarm. He fell from a con-siderable height. He had a huge gash in his skull, a fractured col-larbone that protruded through the skin, assorted broken ribs and a badly swollen knee. Jeanne did what she could to make him comfortable while a nurse's aide extracted several hundred stingers with a pair of tweezers.

It was evident that the boy's condition demanded emergency treatment by a physician. Mairhi, having just returned from Nairobi, was obliged to repeat the long, bumpy ride with Jeanne beside her in the cab of the Land Rover. The injured youth, supported by his father and Albert, one of the mission workers, rode on the jump seats behind them. The fearful head injury ruled out the use of analgesics, but Mairhi injected antihistamine to counteract the dan-gerous amount of bee venom the patient had absorbed. The jolting of the vehicle on the rutted roads caused the young man great agony, but he made no complaint.

A monsoon was developing. The road was soon deep in mud that caused the truck to skid so wildly that it was all Mairhi could do to keep it in the tracks. After an eternity on the muddy road they arrived at the Presbyterian Hospital, only to have their patient refused admittance for reasons that were not made clear. Through darkening skies, deafening claps of thunder, great daggers of lightning and sheets of rain, they continued another fifteen miles to Kenyatta Hospital in Nairobi. There they had to locate a stretcher for themselves and carry the patient inside. Mairhi grimly argued with the staff for twenty minutes before the patient was reluctantly admitted. The resident physician assigned him to a bed but insisted he could stay only one night.

The two women drove back to Olooseos in the unrelenting storm, with the Land Rover slipping and skidding wildly. They arrived very late, worn out, starved and chilled to the bone by rain that found its way into the cab through many leaks. Denny and Lowrie, who had started out in the combi to look for them, had seen the approaching headlights and were waiting at the mission entrance.

The next day, the father of the injured young man appeared again at the mission, this time alone. True to his word, the admitting physician had discharged the patient after a single night. Father and son were returning by bus, but at Keserian, where the injured youth could no longer endure the jolting ride, the father had left him under a tree and walked on alone to Olooseos. Mairhi and Jeanne arranged temporary convalescent quarters and dispatched the Land Rover to Keserian to pick up the patient.

On the last Sunday of September (was it possible that they had been at Olooseos only a month?) there was a farewell party for Samuel Pulei, soon to depart for an extended period of instruction at Queen's College, University of Birmingham. Denny and Jeanne were, of course, invited. Tea, sandwiches and biscuits were served, and there was a great deal of speech-making. Samuel, the object of this celebration, looked dignified in his dark suit and polished shoes. He stood quietly on the crumbling porch of his dilapidated house, which termites seemed intent on demolishing. His wife and children remained shyly in the doorway. There were gifts (a brief-case from the African Church headquarters, a suitcase from the Grindalls and a new pair of shoes from the Andersons) which the pastor accepted with obvious appreciation.

Denny and Jeanne took the opportunity to get better acquainted with this quiet man to whom they found themselves so strongly attracted. After the customary well-wishes, Denny said, "We are thinking of coming back to work with your people. Perhaps some day you can join us." A broad smile broke across the Maasai cler-gyman's face. "If God wills it," he said softly. "that would make me very happy."

Time just flew by after Samuel's farewell party. Suddenly it was time for Denny and Jeanne to go home. A few odds and ends remained to be cleaned up, but for the most part their major un-dertakings had been completed. Chief Moses declared that the Grindalls had accomplished more in three months than others had achieved in ten years.

Shortly before their departure came Denny's memorable fifty-fourth birthday celebration, "the best he's ever had," according to Jeanne's diary. Jerusha and Mairhi served a splendid breakfast and gave "Simba" a wall-hanging emblazoned with lions. Jeanne received one of a zebra, her favorite African animal. Lowrie and Margaret presented Denny with an illustrated animal book and an aerial photo of Olooseos.

When it was time for church, the group piled into the Land Rover and drove to Olosho-Oibor, where services were held regularly. The small church was packed with more than 250 people, the men in their soiled blankets and togas and the women in their freshly laundered shukas. The Grindalls were warmly greeted and made to sit in front. Smiling children came running to them, bowing their heads to receive the traditional Maasai touch on the head. Pastor

Adam Matadi* preached in Swahili, and ole Kangu interpreted in Maa.

After church everyone went outdoors for birthday festivities. Benches were carried out and placed in the shade of a wide-spreading acacia. When food was served, Jeanne and Denny managed to pass up the murky-looking tea and the greasy beef and rice in favor of socializing.

As master of ceremonies, Pastor Adam spoke first, followed by several elders who expressed gratitude for the gifts of water, food and other blessings brought by the American couple. Then it was time to present birthday gifts. Mboya, chief of several villages and a noted orator, declared that the guests of honor deserved only the finest and that no gift was as good as a cow. Since Simba was leaving Kenya, though, a lesser offering would have to suffice. He presented a magnificent Maasai spear, which Denny flexed aloft in a convincing imitation of the warrior manner that delighted his audience. The chief of the morans gave him an elaborately figured bullhide shield, explaining that its markings meant it was reserved for use by "a strong young man." His words were sincere, for in Africa, where old age and death come early, physical vigor is associated with stalwart youth. To the Maasai, as they watched Denny labor tirelessly under the hot sun for many hours without pausing to rest, he seemed much younger than he looked. The shield and spear are still two of the most treasured gifts among those Denny has received from African friends over the years.

The festivities continued. An old man came forward with a fly whisk made from a giraffe's tail. Denny tucked it in the back of his belt and performed a hilarious imitation of a giraffe. When one of the women handed him a beaded belt, he gave her a hug, which

* A pseudonym

pleased her immensely, for in Maasai culture, men seldom demonstrate affection for women. Lemayan brought a belt for each of the Grindalls' sons, and a young girl gave them a necklace for their daughter.

Then it was Jeanne's turn to be recognized. Being less familiar to the group than her husband, she had not expected recognition and was touched by the courtesy. Chief Moses commented gallantly that it was admirable for "such an old woman" to come so far with her husband and work so hard for the Maasai people, and he urged the women in the audience to follow her worthy example. Jeanne noted that his "compliment . . . tickled me no end." Then the women filed forward with beads, necklaces, a printed cloth, a belt and a headdress. One of Mboya's wives gave her a calabash and instructed her seriously to serve milk from it regularly to her husband to maintain his strength.

Finally, Pastor Adam, in the manner of one who has saved the best till last, announced that he was honored to present a gift the like of which had been given only once before and then to the donor of seventy steers. He spread before the Grindalls a magnificent zebra skin. This gorgeous pelt now adorns a wall of the Grindalls' home.

Naturally Denny was asked to speak. As a tactful way of closing the festivities, he invited everyone to accompany him to the waterhouse, where he made a brief address, noting that he and Jeanne had come to Maasailand at the invitation of Mr. Lowrie Anderson. Later the Grindalls learned from Jerusha that ole Kangu translated these words somewhat loosely, referring to Lowrie as "that old chap over there without any hair."

A single awkward incident marred this otherwise perfect day. Three White strangers, two men and a woman, were present but had taken no part in the festivities. Noting that they seemed ill at ease, the Grindalls spoke to them and learned that they were Americans. One of the men was a writer doing research on the Maasai tribe. After some chilling remarks about "civilization creeping in," the writer said with a sneer, "Well, Grindall, now that you're getting famous, I suppose you'll be writing a book about how you saved the poor savages from starvation."

"Oh, no," Denny replied genially. "I've got better things to do. I'll leave the book writing to you experts."

Seven
SIX MONTHS IN KENYA
1971

Vaughan Chamness listened with keen interest as the two adventurers described their three-month experience in Kenya. He had reviewed their slides and was helping them organize a presentation that would be made to the University Presbyterian Church congregation.

"I'm amazed at how much you accomplished," he said. "You know, Helen and I were out there the year before you two first visited the Andersons, so I have a pretty good idea what you were up against. My hat is off to you both."

"Well, thank you, Vaughan," Denny replied. Then, with a conspiratorial glance at his wife, he added, "We're thinking about making it an annual event."

"Three months every year?" exclaimed the pastor. "That's wonderful!"

"Actually, six months. You see, our son Paul can tend the store for us, and our other affairs don't need our full-time attention. By spending half of each year here, we can stay on top of our business and rest up a bit. In the other six months we can really do some good."

The older man's imagination was fired by this vision. "I can see another advantage to your scheme. I'll schedule appearances for you at local churches when you're home, as many as you care to visit. I'm sure there will be lots of financial contributions for your work."

"We're not very good at asking for money," Denny said dubiously.

"That won't be necessary if I know our people," Chamness assured him. "You just tell your story, and you'll find that Christians everywhere will want to help."

After reflecting in silence for a time the minister added, "You know, folks, there is a question you must decide before we plan fund-raising and other details. Do you want to go out there under 475 or on your own?"

Seeing their puzzled expressions, he explained that the reference was to 475 Riverside Drive in New York, the national headquarters of their denomination. From these offices all overseas missions activities were directed. The Grindalls pondered the clergyman's words, then asked for more details.

"If you go out under 475," Chamness explained, "you will be funded by the national church and act as its authorized agents. There is a certain amount of power and security in that arrangement, as you can appreciate. On the other hand, your funding will be limited according to what is allotted to your work, and you can only engage in authorized projects. And, of course, you'll have to submit reports, follow procedures—all that sort of thing."

Denny looked dubious. "This all sounds pretty strange. We weren't thinking of going as missionaries, you know, just neighbors . . . world neighbors, if you like. I'm not much good at paperwork, Vaughan, and when I get started on something, I don't like to be held up."

Chamness smiled. "I thought you would say that. I really think you'll do much better going out on your own. You can count on us here to help you all we possibly can. This is going to be one of the most exciting ministries of our church; I can feel it in my bones."

                                *   *   *

Industrial Birmingham, with its smoking factory chimneys, traffic din and drab, close-packed tenement houses, was an alien, cheerless place to a Maasai accustomed to the space and serenity of East Africa. The homesick Samuel Pulei was able to endure it only by immersing himself in study, prayer and his Bible. Even so, his heart remained heavy. His room was the cheapest, smallest, coldest and dingiest within walking distance of Queen's College. To escape its gloom he studied daily at the college library. He would have taken his books outside except for the continual bad weather.

Even the mail brought only a monthly postcard, for his wife, Edith, had to spend every shilling he could send her to feed the children and buy charcoal for the cooking fire. The only other correspondence that came his way were occasional official communications from the African Church.

On one particularly gloomy afternoon when rain streaked the grimy tenement windows, he found an envelope under the door of his room. The stamp and postmark were unfamiliar; the letter was from the United States, the first of its kind he had ever received. It was from the American man and woman he had met at Olooseos. As he read, the heaviness of his heart was replaced by a buoyancy he had not known since leaving Africa.

The Grindalls had decided to spend half of each year in Kenya, working to help the Maasai people. They planned to arrive in Kenya sometime in June. Would he join them at the Olooseos station and share in this work? Samuel's spirit soared. The letter was to him a message directed by God's own hand. For more than twenty years he had dreamed and worked and struggled toward a single goal: the same goal that this American couple had in mind. He poured out his joy in a prayer of thanksgiving, then hastily dashed off and mailed a reply, promising to cut short his studies and return to Africa as soon as possible.

After his letter was in the mail, a disturbing thought occurred to Samuel. As an ordained minister of the African Church, he was not really free to go dashing home early and to launch some new endeavor. He was expected to complete the course of study in which he was enrolled, then return to his pastoral duties at Moranga.

Doubts assailed him during the days that followed. Then another letter arrived, this one from the headquarters of the African Church. It directed him to conclude his studies at once and return to Nairobi for reassignment to the Olooseos mission, where he was to assist in social and pastoral work among his own tribe.

Tears filled his eyes as he read these words. God was good.

*   *   *

The Grindalls found a huge welcoming party waiting for them when their plane landed at Nairobi airport. The entire Olooseos staff (the Andersons, Mairhi, Jerusha, the Chakans, Joram, Hezron and David) plus a sizeable delegation of robed, beaded and ocher-painted Maasai from Olosho-Oibor were on the concourse platform. They were waving, shouting greetings and jumping excitedly. They hurried through customs and immigration; then the welcoming party descended on them. There was much hugging, kissing and yelling in English, Maa and Swahili before they could board the Land Rover with their luggage and go tearing off for lunch. Overwhelmed, Jeanne recorded in her diary that "we felt like king and queen."

As they drove out to the station they were thrilled by the beauty and harmony that East Africa always displays after abundant rains. The grass was lush, the trees dense with foliage, the cattle sleek and the wild animals exuberant. The abundance of game was astonishing. Herds of impala and Grant's gazelle gamboled friskily; topi, eland and zebra grazed contentedly; Maasai giraffe loped companionably beside the Land Rover, seeming to join in the joyous welcome.

At Olooseos there were more outpourings of affection. Margaret had prepared a dinner fit for royalty. David presented Jeanne with a huge gourd of milk, "greenish and full of specks," which left her hands smelling of smoke even after washing. Samuel Pulei, recently returned from England and assigned to the station, greeted them with a broad smile and warm words of welcome.

There were many changes in evidence at Olooseos. The clinic had a new inpatient unit, equipped to care for premature births, which were a frequent occurrence among the Maasai. Construction of the church was progressing nicely, though Jeanne was a trifle dismayed by the vermillion cross and window frames.

Not all the surprises were agreeable. At Olosho-Oibor Denny turned on a faucet and got nothing. He inspected the pipeline and found a section high on the hillside where the presence of rock had obliged him to leave a length of pipe exposed. Here water spouted from a puncture obviously made by a spear. Resignedly, Denny mended the line with a section of new pipe.

At the earliest opportunity, Denny challenged the elders with a new project. He proposed to build a much larger dam below the existing reservoir. It would provide ample water for cooking, laundering, bathing, watering the animals and irrigating the expanded shamba that he planned to put in. It would also keep the water-intensive dip tank supplied. This was a concrete tank installed by the government in which the Maasai cattle, goats and sheep had to be "dipped" (actually, driven through) weekly in order to keep them reasonably free of disease-bearing ticks that otherwise would sap an animal's strength and make it easy prey to predators. The tank was filled with a strong chemical solution. It had to be drained and replaced every few months, due to thickening and pollution from the filth deposited by the animals.

Denny explained that this new dam would be built of soil and rock, which would be a much cheaper design than last year's concrete dam. Nevertheless, it would cost considerably more because of its vastly greater size, so the men must be prepared to sell more cattle if they wanted this salangi sabok.

Again there arose both loud opposition and vigorous support for Denny's plan. Clearly, some of the tribesmen were disappointed by the return of the meddlesome "European." (Many Africans label all Whites as "European.") A toothless elder named Letawan, ragged and covered with lice, pounded the ground with his cattle stick and shook his head obstinately.

"We should not do this foolish thing. The rains have been good. Engai is generous. Our cows are fat and our goats plentiful. We do not need to sweat under the hot sun digging holes in the ground to please this stranger. It is better to sit under a tree guarding our herds and behaving like proper Maasai."

Some of the men nodded agreement, but most scowled their disapproval. Letawan was not a respected figure in the clan, and his opposition may actually have worked to Denny's advantage. On the other hand, Samuel, who was present as translator, was held in universal esteem, and his advocacy helped weigh the final decision in favor of proceeding with the project.

A Maasai youth with a prized goat

Installing a drain system

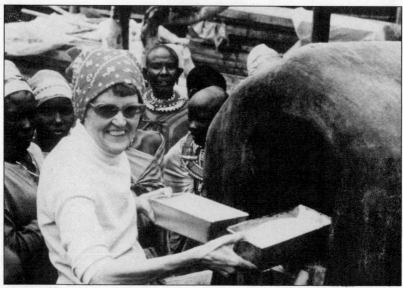

Jeanne and her cooking class bake bread

Denny with Sakatium (Peter) and Kakua (on the right)

Chief Simeon (left, back to the camera) oversees fence construction

An evangelist uses music to instruct young boys

Chief Mboya (Simeon) addresses a council of elders

Maasai warriors

Completed Maasai homes, designed by Denny

Samuel, Simeon and Denny confer on dam construction

Heavy equipment and manual labor are combined to build the crucially needed dam

The Grindalls with Mary Sekuda, Simeon's daughter

Denny and Lainkini with Karaposho looking on

The Reverend Samuel Pulei

During this council, Denny also brought up the matter of vandalism to the pipeline. "Maasai," he said gravely, "your herd boys are undoing the hard work we did last year by making holes in the pipe to get a drink of water. This must be stopped, or there will be no water here at the village. The shamba will dry up, and your children will be sick again."

The elders promised to put fear in the hearts of the herd boys. For a time the threat of severe beatings discouraged vandalism, but gradually thirst overcame discipline, and the boys again began piercing the plastic pipe. Each time, the consequences were severe. Repair involved climbing the hill several times to close the valve at the dam, bleed air from the pipeline, remove the damaged section and insert new pipe. Eventually Denny was forced to replace all the exposed sections with galvanized steel pipe.

An African cattle sale is an important public event. Because of their traditional unwillingness to sell cattle, the Maasai were not experienced in such commerce, but they learned quickly. The men selected 150 of their best steers. They drove them to the designated place, a pole corral about twenty miles away. Denny accompanied them on the drive. He wanted to take pictures and observe the action. Maasai from other clans also came to watch and asked what the herdsmen were doing with their cattle. "We are going to sell them," they said. "With the money we get, we are going to build a salangi sabok so large that we will never again be without water." Some of the onlookers were impressed. Others smiled skeptically.

The site Denny selected for the new dam was a huge wash, just below the concrete dam, that had been scoured from the hillside by torrential rains. Lacking an engineer's education, he could only apply common sense, practical experience and familiarity with the many construction projects he had observed over the years to analyze what needed to be done. By using last year's modest system as a standard, he knew that to increase the quantity of water it would be necessary to increase two other things: volume and pressure. Increasing volume simply meant making a larger dam. Pressure was another matter. Without power to drive pumps, he would have to depend on gravity to supply pressure. This meant locating his dam on the mountainside, even if it was not the easiest construction site or the most suitable place to impound water. All things considered, the dry wash offered the only practical solution.

Although the scope of the project and the amount of labor involved were much greater than on last year's dam, the technology was simpler. The reservoir was to be a basin, roughly circular in shape, scooped from the hillside with shovels. The excavated material would form the semicircular wall on the downhill side.

Denny worried about the possibility of a washout due to erosion from heavy rains and the hooves of animals. Engineers use rock imbedded in the earth embankment, called "riprap," to minimize such risks. At his designated site, however, the quantity of rock available fell far short of what was needed. He began casting about for a nearby source. High on the slope above the dam site, near the crest of the Ngong Hills, was a massive jumble of rock, possibly the result of an earthquake, that was ideal for riprap; however, it lay fifteen-hundred feet above the dam site on a steep, rugged slope, inaccessible by truck. Manual conveyance would be too slow; besides, asking the men to haul the stones downhill one by one in their hands would be unreasonable. Denny resorted to his favorite tactic: turning an onerous task into a contest.

Although by tradition strongly disinclined to labor with their hands, the Maasai are by no means physically indolent; on the contrary, they are great natural athletes who glory in exertion, especially that which gives expression to their penchant for high-spirited, hilarious competition. With this in mind, Denny purchased four wheelbarrows in Nairobi and organized the men into teams of four. Each team's objective was to deliver the largest pile of stones to the dam site each day.

Day after day, the wheelbarrows bounced down the hillside at breakneck speed. The drivers desperately held on while their assistants tried frantically to keep the rocks from flying out along the way. Often, the more exuberant competitors arrived with nothing to show for the trip, while their more cautious opponents scored winning points.

As the earthen wall took shape, it was lined with eighteen-hundred tons of firmly compacted rock. Today the dam is still protected by that same rock. The four wheelbarrows did not fare so well. At the end of the project all were total wrecks.

Some administrative headaches were inherent in the expanded activities. By agreement with Lowrie, Denny segregated the costs of his Olosho-Oibor garden and water projects from the mission station expenses. Revenues from the cattle sale, though impressive, fell far short of covering the cost of pipe, pipe fittings, lumber and other materials. Thanks to the generous support of UPC and several other churches in western Washington, Denny no longer found it necessary to reach deep in his own pocket to augment the Maasai funds, but it was still necessary to keep strict accounts and move money often from the United States to Kenya. Sadly, banking and bookkeeping consumed time that could have been better spent planting vegetables and directing the laying of the pipeline.

Transportation was another nagging problem. Denny's hard-driving schedule kept the station truck tied up much of the time, to the farm manager's continuing annoyance. Aware of this tension source, Denny told Jeanne, "We need a truck of our own out here."

They discussed these difficulties at length. Although their relations with the Andersons remained as warm as ever, Denny's increasing involvement outside the mission was complicating, if not actually competing, with the Olooseos work. What was needed, they concluded, was to create an efficient organization at home to support their special projects. Jeanne proposed the name "Maasai Action for Self-Improvement," or MASI. "You've always said we should not just help them, but help them help themselves," she said. "We ought to get that idea into the name."

Denny liked the name as well as the concept. "But there's nothing we can do about it now," he sighed. "I'll mention it to Vaughan next time I write. Maybe he can get something started before we go home."

On the first Sunday after their arrival, the Grindalls were driving to Olosho-Oibor to attend church when they encountered several Maasai war parties moving along the road. The experience was both fascinating and unnerving, for these young men were very different from the cheerful workers at Olooseos or Denny's merry work crew. They were scantily clad, most wearing only a brief skirt about the loins, and their bodies were garishly adorned with red ocher and chalk tracings. All carried spears. Thigh bells and ankle rings jingled as they trotted along. They glared suspiciously at the passing vehicle.

The third party they met barred their way with outthrust spears. The warriors circled the Volkswagen combi, thrusting their ocherous heads in through its open windows and scowling at its occupants. The odor of their sweating bodies was overpowering. A giant with a heavy scar angling down his cheek barked harsh, threatening words in Maa. Young David answered in the same language. The warriors conferred among themselves for a time, then, with surly scowls, impatiently motioned for the combi to proceed.

"He say somebody steal cows this way," David explained. "They think maybe we do it."

Jeanne allowed herself to breathe again. "I'm glad you convinced him that we aren't rustlers, David," she said fervently.

Not long after this incident Samuel informed Denny that a great assembly of warriors was to take place on the last day of the month at a distant manyatta. Representatives of many clans, some from far away, would gather to compete in contests and celebrate their Maasai manhood.

"Some people say it will be the last. I hope so. They are bad."

Denny wanted to witness the event, the more so because such a ceremony might never be seen again. Samuel assured him there would be many other spectators and agreed to accompany him to Ewaso, where the celebration was to take place.

Not long ago the morans were the heart and soul of Maasai culture. Songs were sung and tales told to children about their courage and pride. When a group of warriors was near, the villagers had no fear of intruders or marauding beasts, and when work was to be done that called for strength and bravery people would say, "What, are there no warriors around today?" Whether the task was branding an unruly bull, tracking and killing a thieving leopard, subduing a rogue rhino or driving off human enemies, it was well known that Maasai warriors would not shirk their duty.

Although usually victorious in battle, the Maasai warrior was also realistic, acknowledging the possibility of defeat. With a shrug he would say, "The war will be won by us or by our enemies" and go into battle singing:

God, bird of prey,
Accompany me on the raid,
Because if I don't get killed, I will kill,
And you will always have one of us to feed upon.

By 1971, however, changes were coming fast, even in Maasailand. Kenya gained its independence in 1963. The following year, Jomo

Kenyatta became its first president. A wise statesman and a strong, even-handed leader, Kenyatta discouraged inter-tribal friction by instituting as a national slogan the loggers' cry "Harambee!" which means "All pull together!" Under this policy, much of the warrior activity was officially out of favor. By 1971, the morans were generally regarded as nothing more than roving gangs of young thugs.

When Samuel and Denny arrived at the manyatta, several hundred other spectators were already on hand, squatting in the grass or lounging in the shade of acacia trees. Soon a squad of warriors came marching down the road, its approach announced by shrill blasts on a decorated kudu horn. As other groups arrived and all began to congregate, it was a spectacle to stir the blood: raw, savage and primitive, yet undeniably beautiful. To the nerve-tingling accompaniment of the kudu horns they came, their bright-colored togas streaming open to display dark, athletic bodies decorated with ocher and chalk tracings. All wore short, Roman-style swords at their waists and carried broad-blade spears proudly upraised. Every man was adorned in all the finery to which his accomplishments and status entitled him. Each warrior who had killed a male lion wore the mane fastened to his head in a style similar to the bearskin busby of a British guardsman. An even more imposing headdress, seen on only a few, was a huge circle of black ostrich feathers framing the face, towering nearly two feet above the warrior's head. As members of many clans arrived, Denny noted that each unit was distinguishable by color and cut of the toga, by elaborate hair styling, by the intricate patterns painted on their buffalo-hide shields and by the fantastic design of their leg tracings.

Each group was accompanied by a covey of small girls . . . bare-chested (but too young to have bosoms). On their clean-shaven heads they wore beaded circlets. Pendulous ornaments dangled from their ears, and around each slender neck was a necklace of colored beadwork so enormous that it all but covered the wearer's shoulders. These were the girlfriends of the warriors, Samuel explained with evident disapproval. They were not supposed to live in the manyatta with the warriors, but they spent most of their time there anyway.

Soon the games and contests began. There were mock battles with green sisal [hemp] stalks as weapons and spear-throwing matches with thick mats of woven grass as targets. A favorite game, creating great hilarity, was a joust between the sexes, with leafy boughs used for switching opponents' torsos, legs and bottoms.

The most impressive display of athletic ability was the jumping event, which was performed with all the ritual of a ceremonial dance. One by one, each contestant entered a wide circle of competitors to show off his prowess. As a test of endurance, he leaped repeatedly in the air as high and for as long as possible, with no visible sign of effort. Hands at his sides and a negligent smile on his lips (to signify the ease of his feat), each warrior sprang again and again, rapidly, to astonishing heights. At the apex of each leap, he shook his shoulders slightly in an apparently stylized way. Each contestant's effort was observed closely by the circle of warriors, who offered encouragement or derision, depending on their allegiance.

As the day advanced, the activity of the warriors became noticeably wilder and less controlled. Denny observed that many, if not all, were chewing something, which Samuel explained was the narcotic bark of a local tree. From time to time one of the men would be seized by an apparent emotional frenzy, accompanied by moaning, rolling of the head and eyes, foaming at the mouth and falling on the ground. Although others attempted to support or restrain the afflicted one, their efforts did little good. The ceremony was taking on a violent, primitive quality that disturbed Denny and Samuel. Quietly, they took their leave.

Once again Jeanne was appointed nurse's assistant and chief bookkeeper at Olooseos. To her dismay, someone had revised the bookkeeping again. "I don't think I'll ever catch on," she confided unhappily to her diary.

The medical cases at the clinic were as numerous, varied and desperate as before: children with measles, croup and diarrhea; battered wives; a youth hemorrhaging and near death from an artery severed during circumcision; a woman cursing hysterically because her infant grandchild had to be rushed to a hospital incubator for oxygen (the child arrived too late and died, confirming the old woman's conviction that hospital care was lethal); broken bones; tropical ulcers; malnutrition; polio; leukemia; gonorrhea; malaria; pneumonia; a man covered with sores from a fall into a tank of cattle dip. Through it all, Jeanne rarely heard a child cry or an adult complain.

July was unusually cold, damp and disagreeable. Jeanne spent most of the month in bed with a heavy chest infection, which she eventually conquered with a massive injection of penicillin.

The dam was completed. It waited to be filled by summer rains. Maasai from as far away as Tanzania came to marvel at this amazing project. At each such visit, Denny was obliged by the demands of his crew to take off his shirt and display his hairy torso. This excited as much interest among the visitors as did the new dam. Simba's fame was spreading throughout Maasailand. After being formally invested as an elder of Chief Mboya's clan, he began calling himself "Denny Simba Maasai," to the immense delight of his fellow clansmen.

Their trust in Denny grew steadily, but the elders still strenuously challenged each new proposal. Although some of the objections seemed to him trifling or groundless, Denny was of course obliged to respect them. He stumbled upon a phrase that served him well in these discussions. With mock gravity he would say, "This plan will work, Maasai. It is of the latest American design." Although the men quickly sensed that he was poking fun both at himself and at them, they often assented to schemes "of latest American design."

When the men asked to have a watering trough built near the new reservoir for their cattle and goats, Denny designed a forty-foot-long concrete structure, two feet high and two feet across with walls six inches thick. As the job got under way, the usual kibitzing commenced. "Too high!" "Too low! "The cattle won't like it!" "Are you sure it will work?" Nevertheless, they proceeded with the work. When the trough was finished, the cattle proved less trusting than their owners. At first they bolted and had to be dragged back with ropes, but with a bit of persuasion, they soon found the strange-looking structure completely satisfactory.

Jonah said admiringly, "Simba, this cattle trough of latest American design is truly the greatest thing we have seen!"

Bringing the much larger volume of water to the village posed greater technical difficulties and increased cost. Laying two miles of galvanized pipe in order to withstand the estimated fifty pounds of pressure was far more challenging than last year's project. Instead of simply following the contours of the ground, as they had done with the smaller line, it was necessary to dig trenches in some places and construct trestles in others. They also had to protect the pipeline from damage by animals, vandals or falling trees. The men worked hard: hacking brush, digging ditches, hauling pipe and clearing away boulders and dead trees.

Meanwhile, water was slowly rising in the dam. When they reached the foot of the hill, Denny decided to encourage his crew with a demonstration of water pressure. He signalled for the valve at the upper end to be opened as the crew gathered around, watching intently. A muffled sound came from within the pipe. Denny checked the pressure gauge. It read one hundred and ten pounds. He opened the valve, and a column of water shot thirty feet in the air. The men were drenched immediately. For an instant, they were too shocked to react; then, laughing and shouting wildly, they jostled each other to get under the refreshing spray.

Denny watched his new friends discover something he had always taken for granted. He realized that no words of persuasion from him would have convinced these men of the benefits of hygiene as well as this, the first shower of their lives.

Once the pipeline reached the valley floor, the work went more easily. The men worked hard, conscious that Denny's departure was drawing near. When they reached the village, he constructed a small waterhouse, framed with saplings and roofed with thatch for insulation, to house a 2,000-gallon storage tank. He designed a simple drinking fountain and, forgetting about the pressure, invited a girl to try it. When she bent to drink, water shot up her nose, leaving her gasping and sputtering. Denny realized that even this simple procedure would have to be taught.

Samuel Pulei's new duties involved outreach and community development at nearby Maasai villages. His immediate superior, the Reverend Adam Matadi, was both board chairman of the Maasai Rural Development Center (that is, Olooseos) and pastor of the nearby parish of Ngong. In both capacities, he was under the direction of the African Church headquarters. From the outset of his new assignment, Samuel was troubled by his superior's apparent disfavor, which he attributed to Matadi being a Kikuyu and he, Samuel, being a Maasai. He worked hard to win Matadi's good will, but still the puzzling coolness persisted.

Still, nothing could dim Samuel's joy at being back with his wife and children. His happiness was intensified by his association with the Grindalls and by the answer to his prayers to work with his people. Although he was very poor and his small house was so decrepit that it scarcely provided a shelter from the elements, now he could at least hope to improve his family's condition by his own labor. He planted a shamba. He also raised some chickens so he would have eggs and meat to sell. God would provide, he assured Edith.

Lowrie and Margaret Anderson were in the final year of their ministry, for on his next birthday, his seventieth, Lowrie would reach mandatory retirement age. Although life at Olooseos was as hectic as ever and their duties unrelenting, the doughty old pair met each new challenge with the verve and energy of youngsters. Increasingly, they invited the Grindalls to share Sunday dinner at "the manse." These were precious times for both couples. After the table was cleared, Lowrie would lead in singing old hymns of the faith, roaring out the words in his strong baritone voice. Later there would be good talk and table games until bedtime. As the hour of their last Sunday evening grew late, Lowrie's mood turned serious. We'll be parting soon, dear friends," he said, "and we won't be seeing much more of each other. But we'll keep you in our prayers, and we know you'll keep us in yours. We can't stop praising God for the miracle of your joining us here. In fact it's our hope that you two will replace us here. I've put the matter before the board of directors. They have some other avenues to explore, but they want you to come out next year as interim directors. I hope you will accept."

After a brief discussion, Denny and Jeanne agreed, and so it was decided.

Obviously, a ceremony was in order to inaugurate the new water system. Interest throughout the district was intense, for the dedication of Chief ole Moiko Dam was easily the most important event to take place in the valley of Olosho-Oibor up to that time. Moses ole Moiko's authority, which extended well beyond the Olosho-

Oibor district, came through government appointment rather than tribal election, so Denny's choice of a project name ensured attendance by all the officials of the area. They arrived in a caravan of limousines, Land Rovers and four-wheel-drive vehicles. The people from the seventeen villages of Olosho-Oibor were present en masse.

The spectators sat on the ground. Chief ole Moiko delivered a long speech, noting that the event marked the first time local Maasai had ever enjoyed such an abundance of water. Samuel interpreted in English for the benefit of the Grindalls. While the people picnicked on milk from their calabashes and meat sliced from a broiled goat, Denny's crew erected a large sign on the bank of the dam. It read:

Chief ole Moiko Dam
1971
God's grace to a Maasai chief
made all this possible.
Built by Olosho-Oibor Maasai men and Denny
Simba Maasai with no government help.
Paid for by Maasai selling cattle,
help from Christians in western Washington, U.S.A.,
and the African Church.
"Dry seasons shall no longer plague these Maasai."

Eight
A LARGER
VISION
1972

F or several reasons 1972 was a watershed year in the Grindalls'
new career. Trial and error had confirmed to them the direction in
which they should proceed. By now they had secured the confi-
dence of the Maasai people and were fully confident in themselves.
Financial donations earmarked for the Maasai work were flowing
into UPC, and public support for their Kenya project rose rapidly.
Lowrie and Margaret, now happily retired, were urging Denny and
Jeanne to tell their story to the Andersons' church in Pennsylvania,
where the Maasai connection had originated. Most important, their
vision of what could and should be done was expanding.

The Grindalls were convinced that sanitary and dietary deficien-
cies were the greatest enemies of the Maasai people. Unless these

problems could be corrected, the Maasai would decline to the point of ultimate extinction. They had some reservations about the mission experiment, for the Maasai, though curious, showed no inclination to imitate the Olooseos model. The benefits, though, that had been achieved at Chief Mboya's village were beyond dispute. Sickness had dropped by fifty per cent in one month after clean water had been piped to the village. Improvements could still be made, however, and what good were the gains made in one village to the people in others?

Concluding that they must expand their range of activity and still maintain some realistic limit on its scope, they began to consider as their target area the entire valley of Olosho-Oibor. This district was roughly twenty miles square and encompassed seventeen villages. Denny then set an ambitious three-part goal for 1972: (1) developing a much larger water supply that would ultimately serve all seventeen communities, (2) increasing by a factor of ten the size of the shamba, and (3) starting construction of a model village that would retain as much as possible of the Maasai way of life while eliminating, or at least reducing, the flies, vermin and bacterial enemies that plagued the villagers.

The Rift Valley is so arid and its subsoil so porous that a permanent water table is in most places nonexistent; therefore, wells, no matter how deep, are unproductive. Ironically, rainfall, though sparse and irregular, sometimes comes in torrential volume. The result is that billions of gallons of precious water rush through *wadis* (dried-up stream beds) and ravines to the Indian Ocean, leaving only a tiny fraction to evaporate quickly in the *kiti salangis*. Denny Grindall realized that only by capturing much more of this wasted rainwater could he hope to meet the most basic of the people's needs. On the valley floor below the hillside location of Chief ole Moiko Dam, he had noted a shallow depression, broad and long, that sloped gently to the south for about two miles. He envisioned closing the lower end at its narrowest point to create a lake of substantial capacity. This vision continued to occupy his thoughts until at length the idea grew into a plan.

He was aware that such an undertaking posed formidable difficulties, but he did not know precisely what those difficulties would be. Of course machinery would be needed, for the project would be many times larger than ole Moiko. He knew that earth-moving equipment could be rented in Nairobi, but it would be expensive; therefore, money would be a prime requisite. He realized also that he would have to design, as well as direct, the building of this huge reservoir, and he was well aware that he did not possess the scientific knowledge that he would need to undertake such a task, for he would be dealing with elemental forces of prodigious power, for destruction and for good, and to do so without undue risk, he must know a great deal more about dam construction. He wrote to the engineering department of the University of California and the Federal Bureau of Reclamation, requesting all available data on the construction of earth dams. He spent long hours poring over these instructions.

Meanwhile, more church appearances were being arranged by Vaughan Chamness, who was now retired and able to devote all his time and talents to the Grindalls' project. He developed and enlarged the best of their photographs, created posters, wrote letters, made telephone calls, collected donations and generally served as unpaid manager, promoter and property man. Through his coaching, Denny and Jeanne were able to make their presentations more polished and interesting. The resulting, generous donations soon made it possible for Denny to buy the truck he wanted . . . a sturdy new Toyota pickup.

Vaughan Chamness began urging them to extend the range of

their appearances beyond the Puget Sound area. "You know, folks," he said earnestly, "we need to interest more lay Christians in doing the sort of things you two are doing, especially those nearing retirement. People in this blessed country of ours are living longer these days, and most have skills and resources that are desperately needed in hard-pressed, undeveloped countries. Think how much good could be done if we could inspire some of them to do the sort of things you are doing."

His urgent words recalled the invitations from Lowrie and Margaret. They wrote their old friends, agreeing to appear at the Andersons' church in Pennsylvania. Vaughan Chamness made the necessary arrangements.

The Beverly Hills Presbyterian Church in Upper Darby, Pennsylvania, under the leadership of Dr. Roy Grace, had already acted on a request from Lowrie and Margaret to transfer financial support from the Andersons' former work in Africa to the Grindalls' Maasai ministry. The congregation was especially enthusiastic about this idea, for it was this same church's concern for the Maasai people, long before Lowrie and Margaret came to Olooseos, that led to the station's development.

Some years earlier a lady member of the Upper Darby congregation read a book about the Maasai people of East Africa. Intrigued, she reviewed the book before the Womens' Guild of her church. The ladies of the Guild were moved by the pathetic conditions of these colorful people and began to pray that God would show mercy to the threatened tribe. It was shortly thereafter that Chief ole Moiko had his encounter with a wandering evangelist that led to the chief's conversion and, through his influence, to the Maasai gift of Olooseos to the African Church.

The reunion with Lowrie and Margaret was joyful, and the presentation to their church a notable success. In his introduction

Lowrie paid them a very special tribute. "In our forty years in the
Sudan," he declared, "Margaret and I were not able to accomplish
as much for the people there as these two have done for the Maasai
in less than a year."

Not all who attended these presentations were favorably disposed
toward the Grindalls' work. There were some dubious looks and
disapproving frowns, and a few asked them bluntly, "Do you really
think it's right for you to change people's lives so drastically?" They
did their best to respond to these doubters, but some remained
unconvinced.

"If only they could see a Maasai village," Jeanne sighed, "they
would understand why the people have to change."

When such criticisms were raised in Kenya, they were able to
arrange visits and let the critics see for themselves the pathetic
conditions of the Maasai. In all such cases Jeanne's prediction
proved true: those who were originally the most skeptical became
some of the Grindalls' staunchest supporters.

The Grindalls discussed with the members of their support group
at the University Church their idea of forming an organization to
facilitate their work in Kenya. Denny, describing the complexities
of international money transfer, recounted some of the frustrations
he had experienced. He explained that if they were to widen their
range of public appearances in accordance with Chamness's plan,
and if doing so should result in increased donations, administration
would soon become unwieldy. There was clearly a need for some
formal structure to manage funds and other details.

The scheme was favorably received by their friends. Several vol-
unteered their services. Among these was Dwight Logan, a certified
public accountant, who suggested establishing a nonprofit corporation with some of the UPC support group as officers. Lawrence
Bailey, a Seattle corporation lawyer, donated his services in setting

up the organization. Everyone liked Jeanne's suggestion of Maasai Action for Self-Improvement (MASI) as a name. Steve Grindall was elected treasurer.

Denny proudly painted MASI on the doors of his new truck.

The mission station property at Olooseos belonged to the African Church, headquartered in Nairobi. Its board of directors was chaired by Adam Matadi. The dozen or so Maasai and Kikuyu workers were employed by the African Church, whereas the volunteers (under the Church's direction)—Colin Crabbee, the new director, nurse Mairhi McRitchie and young Michael McCoy—were employees of the Volunteer Service Organization of Great Britain. The Grindalls, though independent and unpaid, were nevertheless subject to direction by the African Church with respect to all mission activities. As directors of MASI, they were now able to pursue their other interests, that is, their work at Olosho-Oibor, independently.

Samuel Pulei's status was that of an employee of the African Church under the supervision of Adam Matadi, who was also pastor of the Ngong parish. Matadi allowed Samuel to develop and carry out his own work and paid little attention except to criticize Samuel to his own superiors.

On a certain day when Samuel was to receive his monthly salary, none was forthcoming. Thinking it only an oversight, he allowed a few days to pass before bringing the matter up with Matadi. He got an evasive reply, and when another week went by and Samuel again raised a question, Matadi turned him away with an angry rebuff. With a heavy heart, Samuel told Edith what had happened. She burst into tears, and for once Samuel could find no words to comfort her.

The months that followed were desperately difficult for the Puleis. Samuel wrote a letter to the church headquarters in Nairobi and,

while waiting for a response, put himself and his family on a sub-
sistence-level program. He expanded his small garden and raised
more chickens and also rabbits. Meanwhile he continued to petition
the church headquarters for restoration of his salary. During this
period of austerity, his new friends the Grindalls knew nothing
about Samuel's difficulties. They had no way of knowing that their
own activities, and the new truck with the letters M-A-S-I promi-
nently displayed on its doors, were largely responsible.

With Samuel as his interpreter, Denny conveyed his three-part
plan to an assembly of Maasai elders representing the seventeen
villages of Olosho-Oibor. Those not acquainted with the American
knew of his work over the past two years and understood that he
was trustworthy and capable; nevertheless, his proposal seemed
radical . . . even revolutionary. It would cost many cattle and violate
cherished traditions. There were skeptical frowns, shaking of heads
and murmurs of disapproval.

Keenly aware of these obstacles, Denny described an inexhaust-
ible *salangi* that would provide for the needs of all the people and
their herds. It would not dry up when rains failed. He spoke of a
very large *shamba* that would yield wholesome food for their families. Saving the best for last, he promised to help them build clean,
comfortable houses where a man could live out his life and see his
children thrive. Still there remained much opposition.

The nucleus of the dissent was a man who spoke not a word
himself, yet Denny sensed in him powerful animosity. He was a
heavy man of middle age, distinguished by a red stocking cap and
an intent, malignant stare. As the debate raged, his eyes never left
Denny's face. Jonah had identified this elder as *the ol-iburi*, a Maasai
title applied to one skilled in wizardry. He lived apart from the
villages and, when summoned, brought magic sticks and performed
mystic rites that were supposed to drive away evil spirits and heal

diseases. For these services his usual charge was a kid or lamb or, for more serious cases, a young heifer.

Chief Mboya ole Sekuda rose to speak. He was head of the village served by the existing water system and a new convert who had taken the Christian name Simeon. An impressive, even regal figure, well over six feet tall and powerful despite his more than fifty years, Simeon was well aware of the respect he commanded. He was not reluctant to use his power. A member of Denny's work crew, he had, on occasion, avoided tasks that he considered beneath his dignity but seldom missed a day's work. He had toiled as diligently as any. As he spoke, his voice was deep and compelling.

"I have lived longer than most of you and have seen many of our people die, as well as many cattle. My heart has broken when I saw little ones too weak to suck from their dying mothers' breasts. You may do as you decide, but I have turned my back forever on the old, deadly way of life. I will sell ten cows and work with Simba."

It was a good speech, and it swung the majority to Denny's plan. Those who remained opposed and still stubbornly refused to drive their cattle to the auction were warned that they would not be allowed to share in the benefits. The elders recognized, though, that the threat was not enforceable. Most of the holdouts would grudgingly join the work as it progressed, but by their early show of opposition they hoped to spare themselves the anguish of parting with their cows.

Denny's first project was to clear a five-acre garden plot at the site of last year's small shamba. His coworkers were making a radical break from a long-standing tradition. The Maasai have forever scorned all horticulture and looked down on farmers as inferior beings. This may have been the first time that any Maasai man ever put his hands in the red earth and planted seeds in the ground. They went at the work with such enthusiasm that Denny was hard put to prevent cabbages, carrots and turnips from popping up in the same row. He assigned a forty-by-sixty-foot plot to each household, allowing the owner to identify his tract with his own cattle brand or some other distinctive mark.

While this work was in process, others, both men and women, dug postholes, set posts and stretched a twelve-foot-high mesh fence around the perimeter of the garden. Surveying the finished enclosure, Denny assured his crew that no giraffe or impala would reach or leap over this fence of "latest American design."

Under the equatorial sun, in rich, well-watered soil, the new plants sprouted and flourished, nearly doubling in size each day. Then, mysteriously, they began to wilt and die. The villagers shook their heads and looked questioningly at Denny. A quick check revealed that soil termites were eating away the roots. An application of insecticide soon banished the termites. The young vegetables again began to sprout and double in size daily as the gardeners watched with mingled satisfaction and anxiety.

Then disaster struck again. Whole rows of vegetables disappeared in a single night. This time it was plain that the damage had been done by something other than root-boring insects, for the tops of the vegetables had been eaten down to the ground. While studying the problem, Denny observed movement in one of the rows. At his approach, a rabbit hopped away. He realized then that in his preoccupation with making the fence giraffe- and impala-proof, he had neglected to close the bottom. He set his crew to work pinning the bottom down with rocks, and when this was done he felt confident that the shamba was secure. The depredations slowed, but did not entirely stop. Finally it came to him that several rabbits had been trapped inside the fence!

After the rabbit episode there were no more problems, and reseeding soon repaired the damage. The amazing growth rate, plus the size and succulence of the vegetables, more than compensated for the temporary setbacks. Soon they were harvesting carrots, cabbages, cauliflower, brussel sprouts, beets, turnips, broccoli, lettuce, kohlrabi, eggplants and potatoes. Later there would be corn and beans, while in the small greenhouse tomatoes were being started.

The people soon learned to enjoy vegetables raw as well as cooked. Carrots remained a favorite. They also liked kohlrabi and eggplant. Potatoes were popular with everyone.

The daily routine of watering, weeding, cultivating and harvesting fell mainly to the women, as Denny kept the men busy at heavier projects. Denny and Jeanne were fascinated by the styles and techniques the neophyte gardeners applied. Their body postures were especially interesting and typically African.

In America, most vegetable gardeners kneel on the ground or on a cushion as they work. In Asia, peasant farmers crouch on their haunches to tend their rice crops. But the village women of Africa bend stiff-legged from the waist to get close to their vegetable plants, in the same way that they collect twigs, dung or other objects from the ground. The posture is one of unconscious grace and extraordinary flexibility. To Denny and Jeanne there was no more amazing sight than that of a tall, slender Maasai woman bending double, her legs perfectly straight and her chin nearly resting on her knees as she worked delicately among her vegetables. When this image appears in their slide shows in America, it invariably produces an incredulous gasp from the audience, which allows Denny to deliver one of his favorite lines: "I can't do that. I just can't straighten up again!"

In addition to Jeanne's work at Olooseos, she began teaching domestic skills to the women of the villages. She taught them how to prepare and cook vegetables and how to bake bread in the brick oven that Denny built for her. The Maasai, who had never tasted

any of the dishes she introduced, particularly enjoyed her fresh-
baked bread. Tapioca pudding was another favorite, especially with
Simeon, who would devour any quantity of this treat he could get
his hands on.

Many and varied are the details that must be considered in the
design of a large earth dam. All are critical to success, and the
neglect of any can lead to disaster. Denny was satisfied that the site
he had chosen was ideal for his purpose. The dry wadi at the foot
of the hills drained a large area and funneled through a narrow
opening where the presence of rock and hard earth offered solid
moorings for the dam. Trees and brush, scattered thinly across the
floor of the wadi, were easily removable. Best of all, the site was
readily accessible to ten of the seventeen villages of Olosho-Oibor.

Denny rented a bulldozer and earth-mover in Nairobi. The appearance of these massive, noisy machines created great excitement, for none of the villagers had ever seen heavy equipment in
operation. When the operator lowered the bulldozer blade and
pushed aside a boulder that a dozen men could not have moved,
a new era dawned in Maasailand.

One day a vehicle bearing government markings drew up to the
dam site. A Black man, an official by his dress and manner, climbed
out of the car and approached the crew at work. As Denny greeted
the man, he wondered what this man's visit was all about. The
official identified himself as a government engineer. He asked if he
might inspect the dam project.

As Denny explained the project and answered questions, the
visitor showed keen interest. The two men climbed the rocky slope
of the dam and surveyed its impressive height and length and the
long expanse of scoured earth that lay at its foot. The questions
continued. Who was the architect? Denny acknowledged that he
had designed the dam. What was its capacity? Four million gallons.

And the cost? Something under a half-million Kenya shillings ($28,000). Who was funding the project? The Maasai villagers of Olosho-Oibor, with supplementary donations from American Christian groups.

The official ran his eye down the massive wall. Its rim was straight and true, its evenly graded slope imbedded with closely fitted stones. What instruments were used? he wanted to know. Slightly chagrined, Denny admitted that the only instrument used was his carpenter's level. The visitor stared at him in seeming disbelief, then asked to see the engineering blueprints. Denny unrolled a soiled and dog-eared set of drawings, which the official examined wordlessly.

"Very interesting," he said at last, "but I do not recognize your engineering degree." He pointed at the signature in the lower right-hand corner, which read, "Denny Simba Maasai, JOAT." "What does JOAT stand for, please?"

Denny's sunburned face split in a broad grin. "That's for 'Jack of All Trades.' I earned it at the Kenya School of Hard Knocks."

The visitor's official manner relaxed. With a smile as wide as Denny's, he said, "Mr. Grindall, this is the most amazing sight these eyes have ever beheld. With a carpenter's level and a gang of Maasai cattle thieves, you have done what our government engineers have never been able to do. You have done it in only a few months at a cost so low no one is going to believe my report." Taking a card from his pocket, he handed it to Denny. "Keep this. If you ever run into trouble, come and see me." With a nod, he returned to his vehicle and drove away.

With each passing day, the bond between Denny and Samuel deepened and strengthened. Their preoccupation with the work limited most of their conversations to practical details, but occasionally there were moments for reflection. One day as they paused to rest in the shade of a tree, Denny asked, "Have you ever wondered, Sam, how all this could happen? How was it possible for a florist from halfway around the world and a Maasai born in a mud house to have the same dream? And how did we get together and actually start to do it?"

Samuel's dark eyes glowed, "Yes, I think about it all the time, but I do not know the answer. It is just a miracle!"

There can be no habitat worse suited to human health and welfare than a Maasai *engang*. A circle of dark, cramped, nearly airless huts inside an enclosure of thornbrush provide a common shelter for humans and animals. Flies breed by the millions, and fleas, lice and ticks carried in by the animals bring misery and life-shortening diseases. Curiously though, in spite of their constant suffering, the Maasai are happy and enjoy their way of life.

Denny's model village was designed to accommodate the people's attachment to tradition. Among its criteria was the stipulation that it should look as much as possible like the typical Maasai *engang*. He knew that otherwise the elders would never accept the plan. Also, recognizing that the frequent movement of the Maasai people led to many of their health problems, he designed the dwellings for permanence. Permanence would bring schools, churches, clinics and other community developments that were beginning to appear among other tribes. He realized, however, that the Maasai were not alone in refusing to accept the inevitable doom of nomadism.

Just as some Americans of a century ago sought to preserve the free life of the "blanket Indians" who roamed the Western plains and lived in tepees, so also many people today, Africans and non-Africans alike, want the old Maasai ways retained in order to preserve a link with the romantic past. Denny and Jeanne saw this sentiment as selfish and unrealistic; they saw change as both inevitable and essential to Maasai survival. They considered Maasai survival vastly more important than nostalgic sentiment.

Denny laid out an area near the original *engang* as a site for his model village with the assistance of Samuel, Simeon and Jonah. After the men and women cleared away brush and rocks, he directed construction of a circular chain-link enclosure stapled to cedar posts. This area, some three hundred and sixty feet in diameter, defined the location of the new village. A controversial feature of the model village was the segregation of animals from the human habitation. The Maasais' attachment to their cattle was strong, but on this point Denny remained adamant: the cattle, sheep and goats must be sheltered apart from the human dwellings. It was only Simeon's strong support that enabled Denny's wish to prevail.

The Grindalls' impending return to Seattle precluded starting the actual construction of houses. That would have to wait until next year. Nevertheless, Denny began staking out building sites. He laid a waterline that would serve each dwelling as well as the central washroom and laundry. The plan also called for a children's playground, a combined church and meetinghouse, an enclosure for women's classes and a vegetable market. There would, of course, be other refinements as needs became known. The new *engang* was to be called Pulei Village.

The dam was finished and empty. It laid waiting to be filled. Light autumn rains had created a few scattered shallow pools in its floor. Even these were thrilling to the Maasai as they drove their herds and brought their water cans to the *salangi sabok*. The pools were also gratifying to Denny, for they confirmed the effectiveness of the clay with which he had lined the bottom of the reservoir to retard seepage. Before the departure of the Grindalls it was necessary to dedicate the dam with an appropriate ceremony. On a chilly November day Jeanne, wearing a knit suit and perky little hat, and Denny, in a suit and tie, joined the workers and their families. The workers brought their wives and children, all dressed up in their brightest beaded necklaces and most colorful ear ornaments. The ancient elders, wrapped in woolen blankets and with their ever-present cattle sticks, shuffled along behind the capering children.

There were visiting Maasai from distant clans and well-dressed clerical and governmental officials from Nairobi. There were long speeches by ole Moiko and Simeon, still longer speeches from the VIPs and brief addresses by Denny and Samuel. On the wall of the dam a newly planted sign read:

CHAMNESS LAKE
1972

In appreciation to a retired pastor, still working and encouraging others to the mission field. Man-made by progressive Olosho-Oibor Maasai to assure themselves of a better way of life. "They shall neither thirst any more." Paid for by the selling of cattle, help from the African Church and Christians in America. An outreach project of the Maasai Rural Development Center at Olooseos.

Designed by Denny "Simba" Maasai

Nine
PULEI VILLAGE
1973

In a single night of torrential rain, Chamness Lake filled to its spillway. It was April and the Grindalls were in Seattle, so of course they learned of it by mail. Samuel's letter eloquently expressed the wonder and joy of all his people, for the Maasai, having wandered for countless generations in arid lands, had never seen such an expanse of water. It stretched for a mile and a half along the formerly dry wadi, at its widest point spanning half a mile: a veritable inland sea!

The women laughed and chattered as they filled their water cans, heedless now of the few drops spilled on the way back to their villages. The men smiled as they watched their cattle and goats wade to their bellies and drink their fill. At night elephants and wildebeest

came. As time passed, waterfowl never before seen in the area nest-
ed and fed along the lake's irregular shoreline.

When Denny and Jeanne arrived in June, the wonder of Chamness Lake still held its fascination for the people. Chief Simeon
wrapped Denny in a great bear hug and pounded his back joyously,
much to the amazement of the watching Maasai, who had never
seen Black men and White men treat each other so heartily. (During
the colonial era, the races were so rigidly separated that "Europeans"
[Whites] were widely thought to be supernaturally protected from
contact with Africans.)

The Crabbees were still at the mission station, as was Samuel.
Nurse Mairhi McRitchie had returned to Scotland, though, and the
Chakans were in West Germany, where Istvan, no longer welcome
at Olooseos, was delivering a treatise on nomadic life in East Africa.
He was seeking a new assignment to the Sudan. (Years later the
Grindalls learned that Istvan had drowned while attempting to cross
a rain-swollen river.)

Colin Crabbee offered the Grindalls a choice between their previous dwelling and the house vacated by the Chakans. They chose
the former and spent their first day cleaning up what the mice had
overlooked of their stored belongings. A pile of Denny's underwear
and even a pair of his shoes had been chewed beyond salvage. On
a brighter note, they found waiting for them an invitation from some
Maasai friends in Kajiado to come to lunch the following day.

Crossing through Olosho-Oibor on their way to Kajiado, they saw
signs of severe drought. The lion grass appeared not merely dry but
dead. The hills and hollows bore the look of a desert.

The people of Kajiado gave them an exuberant welcome. The
women were vividly made up with ocher, and they were adorned
in their finest beadwork. The young evangelists wore their best
European clothes. A stranger introduced himself as Jacob Kim-

aru;* he informed them that he had been engaged by the Bible
Society to translate the New Testament into Maa. There were children too. Little Jonah inclined his head shyly to receive the traditional Maasai greeting. A youth named Emanuel had grown noticeably in six months and was full of smiles at seeing them again. A
healthy, chortling baby boy was introduced as Denny. His namesake
was honored to meet this newest Maasai. "What wonderful, Spirit-
filled, joyous Christians they are!" Jeanne recorded in her diary.

Chamness Lake attracted many visitors. A group of Maasai elders
walked all the way from Tanzania to see for themselves the miracle
they had heard about. The spectacle seemed somehow dishearten-
ing to their chief, a bent and wizened man in a soiled blanket.

"How lucky you are!" he lamented. "You are fortunate to live here
where you have all this water. Your cattle are sleek and fat, and you
even have water to wash your clothing and bodies. We have nothing."

Chief Simeon's lip curled in scorn. "Listen to me, Maasai. Your
words are like wind. We have what you see because we sold many
cattle and worked in the hot sun, carrying rocks in our hands. If
you are willing to do what we did, you, too, can have these good
things."

Denny affirmed Simeon's words, offering his assistance to the
visitors, but they only shook their heads sorrowfully and walked
away. In all their years in East Africa, the Grindalls were never able
to establish effective contact with the people of Tanzania.

One day, two men appeared at Pulei Village. They strolled around
the compound taking notes and giving every appearance of disapproving of what they saw. Denny approached them and introduced
himself. They gave their names and informed him that they were

---

* A pseudonym

scientists: one an anthropologist and the other an environmentalist.

"I suppose you realize, Mr. Grindall," said the environmentalist coldly, "that you are destroying something very precious here." He pointed to the faucet where the women filled their water vessels. Denny had nailed a sign to the post supporting the pipe. It read "Ye Olde Waterhole."

"What is that?" Denny inquired.

"A vital social institution. When the women fill their vessels at their traditional pools, they mingle with each other socially at the same time. It gives them an opportunity to exchange community gossip and chitchat."

"Well," Denny said mildly, "I've noticed they do that here too."

"But they don't linger as they are accustomed to doing," insisted the anthropologist. "It's no longer a social occasion."

"The reason they linger at their salangis," said Denny, "is because the men won't let them fill their water cans until the cattle have finished drinking. By then the water, which was polluted to begin with, is nothing but mud, urine and feces."

The two men smiled skeptically, nodded and went on their way. They were both clearly of the same mind as when they came.

Samuel was revealing unexpected technical competence, the result of his years at Limuru when he had supported himself as a handyman while attending seminary. He kept the Toyota truck and other mechanical equipment in good running order and safely stored. He quickly taught himself to operate the garden tractor that Denny had sent ahead of his own arrival. He even learned to use its posthole-digging attachment and other sophisticated accessories. In all ways he exceeded the Grindalls' expectations. Samuel and his family still occupied the dilapidated little shack near Olooseos. He augmented his minuscule salary (finally restored after a mysterious eight-month hiatus, but without restitution of the missing payments) by cultivating a shamba and raising chickens for eggs and meat. He received an order from the owner of the Maasai Inn in the town of Ngong for twenty broilers a week at a price of 7.50 shillings per kilo, to be delivered slaughtered and cleaned. By tradition, the Maasai abominate all birds, so poor Samuel had no experience with fowl; moreover, he was too tenderhearted for such bloody work. Denny, drawing on his years in the feed-and-seed business, offered to help. At first they were obliged to kill the birds with a *panga* and use Denny's penknife to remove the entrails. Edith plucked the birds while a hired boy fetched hot water. The proprietor of the Maasai Inn expressed satisfaction and ordered another twenty broilers for the following week. After a faltering start, Samuel was in the poultry business.

In the meantime, relations between Samuel and his superiors continued to deteriorate. Adam Matadi, his supervisor, was drinking heavily and scarcely bothering to conceal his animosity toward the Grindalls and Samuel. To make things worse, Matadi was exerting a strong negative influence on his own superior, Joseph Kariuki,* head of the African Church, with respect to Samuel.

Kariuki had attained his high position in a most unusual way. At the close of the colonial era, he was one of hundreds of natives languishing in prison under suspicion of involvement in the Mau Mau violence against the Whites. Since these accusations were difficult to prove, and since the English realized that Kenya's independence was imminent, the authorities began clearing the prisons. They hoped to create good will and avoid a bloodbath when power changed hands. To satisfy the demands of British justice, some rationalization had to be given for this action. Since many of the Mau Mau atrocities were linked to indigenous religious beliefs, the

---

* A pseudonym

conditions attached to clemency were repentance and conversion. Joseph Kariuki accepted Christianity and walked out of prison a free man.

The Kikuyu are a clever, adaptable people. Throughout the colonial era, they were the tribe most closely associated with the ruling British. This association put them in a favored position to inherit power when the English departed. Kariuki, an eminent Kikuyu and a skillful politician, became, in a remarkably short time, the most powerful church official in East Africa. He was also to play a significant role in the life of Samuel Pulei. One day, not long after Kariuki's elevation to this post, a party of missionaries came to the African Church office requesting assistance. They wanted to visit a traditional Maasai village to take some pictures. Joseph Kariuki was happy to accommodate them. He conducted them to an *engang* not far from the town of Ngong. Approaching confidently, he expected a ceremonious welcome by the chief. Instead, a horde of savages armed with clubs, spears and swords burst out of the thornbrush enclosure, making threatening gestures. The visiting party withdrew in undignified haste.

Although badly shaken, Kariuki did not want his guests to go away disappointed. Recalling that the headmaster of the primary school in the nearby town of Ngong, a Maasai formerly called Ntienput ole Pulei, was, like himself, a recent convert to Christianity, he decided that Pulei might be influential with the unfriendly villagers and therefore useful. He went to this headmaster and requested assistance.

Samuel laughed at Kariuki's story, for he knew that the villagers would never admit strangers except by prior arrangement. He went to the chief of the *engang* and politely requested cooperation. Joseph Kariuki and the missionaries returned, somewhat nervously, and obtained some exceptional photographs.

As Kariuki reflected upon this incident, an idea began to fire his imagination. The experience confirmed that the Maasai were popular with visitors to Kenya but also extremely suspicious of strangers. Tourism, he knew, would be a major industry for years to come, and Maasai village life would be a prime tourist attraction. He was not averse to make himself helpful to wealthy and influential visitors by arranging future tours like the one just completed, but without a contact, an insider known and respected by the tribesmen, their notorious hostility toward outsiders would make close observation dangerous, if not impossible.

It came to him that this humble headmaster, Ntienput ole Pulei (who now called himself Samuel), could be made use of many times over if a way could be devised to exploit him fully. He recalled that Pulei was a man of great piety. Would he not serve better as a clergyman than a schoolteacher? Properly handled, he could be ordained within Kariuki's denomination, subject to the orders of the African Church. He could, in fact, be brought under the personal control of Joseph Kariuki. When Joseph Kariuki proposed to Samuel that he give serious thought to entering the pastoral ministry, Samuel's reaction was one of astonishment and joy, for it seemed a clear confirmation that God was answering his prayer. His relatives and colleagues, however, thought otherwise. They could not understand why a young man who seemed destined for an important place in the new nation would want to bury himself in such a lowly occupation. The parents of his pupils also opposed him, but for a more selfish reason. They wanted their children to continue to benefit from his demonstrated skills as an educator. Samuel turned a deaf ear to all these objections and spent the next four years, 1964 through 1967, at St. Paul Theological Seminary at Limuru. During these years, he proved an excellent student, despite being obliged to work long hours after classes to pay for his tuition and self-support. Despite his heavy workload, there somehow was time for romance, for it was during this period that he met and married Edith.

Samuel was especially influenced by two of his seminary instructors, both Americans. One of them, Dennis Clifford, was also his supervisor on his part-time job at the seminary. It was from this friendly, energetic young man that he learned to drive a tractor, maintain pumps and other machinery, and repair equipment. Later he would recognize in Denny Grindall the versatility and resourcefulness that he had admired in the hardworking Dennis Clifford.

William Anderson taught church history, a subject not greatly appreciated by youthful scholars. Samuel Pulei, a few years older than his peers and serious by nature, enjoyed this subject that other seminarians found boring. It was his scholarship that first brought him to the attention of Mr. Anderson, who then began to perceive the exceptional character of the young Maasai. While spending weekends with his parents, Lowrie and Margaret Anderson, then launching their work at Olooseos, William gave them glowing reports about his star pupil. William suggested that Samuel would be a great asset to Lowrie and Margaret at Olooseos.

Thus was the fabric being woven of the future of Samuel Pulei and the Maasai people when Denny and Jeanne Grindall made their first visit to Kenya. By 1973, though, Joseph Kariuki was having second thoughts about the wisdom of bringing Pulei into the clergy. Adam Matadi was bringing disturbing reports that suggested potential trouble, even schism. Pulei, it seemed, was more interested in the activities of his new American friends than in mission labor. There were even indications that he might be trying to launch his own church. The person who was giving him such notions was that meddling American, Denny Grindall.

On July 9 Denny went with Samuel, Simeon and Jonah to meet

with elders of the community of Saikeri, who had expressed interest in starting a water project like the one at Olosho-Oibor. Denny surveyed the area and found a site that he considered ideal for a large dam. The Saikeri elders and their visitors sat down to talk business.

Jonah spoke first. He said, "I tell you, men of Saikeri, that you will no longer be able to sit comfortably under a tree watching your cattle if you really want to do what we have done. You will have to bend your backs and sweat, and you will have to sell some of your fine cattle to pay for materials and rent machinery."

Then Simeon stood up to speak. The ring of elders took in his dignified bearing and listened respectfully to his words. "Some time ago, during a terrible drought," he began, "our cattle were dying of thirst, and we were suffering great hunger. We had heard of a church that sometimes helped people in trouble, and we asked them to come and help us. They came, and they told us about their God who loves all mankind and about his son Christ, who once came and lived with men and suffered their hardships. We prayed to this God, asking him for the water that we needed. As you have seen, he answered our prayers. I commend this God to you and urge you to receive him so you may also have the things you need."

Among themselves the elders discussed what they had heard at length. Then their chief rose to speak. "We do not hate this God you speak of," he said. "We just don't know anything about him. We would like to hear more. And we are ready to make whatever sacrifices are necessary to have water for ourselves and our animals."

Denny was impressed by the earnestness of this statement, but he was also by now sufficiently experienced in Maasai ways to be wary. He told them that before starting the project he must see that they had in the bank, or in Pastor Samuel's hands, at least 120,000 shillings. He would then go to the equipment renter, who had assured him that he would make available a bulldozer. After further discussion the Saikeri elders agreed to these terms.

Denny was eager to start constructing the model village that he had laid out the previous year. One of the immediate requirements was to provide a suitable place for the teaching of Jeanne's classes. The number of attendees had grown to several hundred, many more than the small church could accommodate. They were currently meeting in the open compound, but the wind, flies and blazing sun made this arrangement difficult. Jeanne had no objection to holding her classes outside if these problems could be overcome.

The eventual solution was a circular enclosure of native design which the Maasai call an *alelacei*. An eight-foot-high wall of sheet metal broke the wind and provided partial shade, and by being located apart from the dwellings it reduced the swarms of flies. It was also an excellent theater for showing films provided by American church groups. With the little Honda generator powering the projector, Denny showed movies on various subjects to an enthralled audience. One film that captured their interest but needed much explanation was of Eskimos hunting seals on an Arctic ice floe.

At six-thousand-feet elevation, Kenya's nights can be chilly even when the days are hot, and in winter, July and August, the days are also cool. The Maasai women wanted to learn from Jeanne how to knit sweaters for their children and themselves, though the men refused to give up their traditional blankets, which they wrapped about their shoulders. From their skill at beadwork, the women easily mastered knitting, though at first Jeanne had to rip out many stitches and have her pupil start anew. Neither they nor she minded, for this provided a way to get better acquainted and to improve language skills. During her shopping trips to Nairobi, Jeanne searched the woolen stores for yarns of the color and weight she felt would be popular with her pupils. Since Kenya is a major wool-producing nation, the selection was excellent.

The dressmaking classes were another big hit. The women were eager to be rid of their traditional *shukas* and goatskin capes in favor of something "more fashionable," as Samuel put it. Jeanne stayed busy cutting out simple patterns. Again, experience in beadwork gave her pupils a good start. Soon they were modeling their own creations and dressing their daughters in the work of their own hands. One day when a little girl came with her mother, Jeanne noticed that the child was wearing her dress inside out. The mother explained that the dress had become soiled during Sunday school, so she had simply turned the clean side out!

Denny was ready to start building houses, the basic units of his model village. They were to be fly-proof, termite-proof, well lighted, airy and comfortable, yet they must look like traditional Maasai houses.

He had created a design that was based on the ferro-cement technology that had fascinated him since his high school days. There would be a simple sixteen-feet-square concrete slab, above which would be a curved shell of concrete similar to a Quonset hut and simulating as closely as possible the traditional loaf shape of a Maasai house. The ends would be framed for doors and windows to provide access, ventilation and light.

He had also developed a financing scheme emphasizing owner responsibility. Each man desiring a house must guarantee the estimated cost of three hundred dollars by agreeing to sell two cows. Of course, he must also share in the work. Chief Simeon, intrigued by the prospect of living out his remaining years in a permanent dwelling, made the first pledge.

By the time work commenced in July, the crew was experienced with concrete, so the first slab was laid expertly. While the concrete was curing, Denny began cutting the forms that would shape the structure. He bent sections of quarter-inch plywood on curved forms, then bolted them together and the whole to the concrete slab. Over the forms he spread reinforcing bar and chicken fencing. Then he set the women to work spreading a rich cement mix over the shell.

Since ancient times Maasai women have collected mud and fresh cow dung, which they spread with their hands over a framework of woven wattles. Who, then, could be better qualified to apply a wet cement mix to this modern Maasai house "of latest American design"? When the women were finished, Denny supervised the placement of wet burlap over the entire structure. For the next five days he made certain that the burlap was kept moist to ensure proper curing. Meanwhile, he directed the framing of the two ends of the building.

When the job was finished, Simeon declared himself thoroughly satisfied. Denny realized at once, though, that the house would be uninhabitable, for the blazing sun turned the interior into a furnace. He cast about for a suitable insulating material and finally settled on the lion grass that flourished in abundance close at hand. At first he tried thatching in the conventional African pattern, but the ceaseless Rift Valley wind tore the grass away as fast as he put it up. Next he tried gluing the grass down with a mastic but was embarrassed by the total failure of this "lousy idea." His third attempt was successful. He stretched lengths of chicken wire on the ground and fastened layers of grass to it, then had each section drawn across the house, wire side up. The result was a delightful "little grass shack," cool and pleasing to the eye. Simeon promptly installed his *enkirotet* (favorite wife) in the new home.

Simeon had at the time four wives, not an uncommon arrangement for a Maasai man of substance. The men of the valley were puzzled by Denny's devotion to a single mate. At first they assumed that he had others in America, but he assured them that such was not the case. Finally, one of the men asked him why he did not take many wives, as a man of his obvious stature was expected to do. Denny replied gently that Jeanne was his only love, that she fulfilled his every need and that it would be unthinkable to share what he felt for her with any other. The Maasai pondered this answer and seemed satisfied.

One fine Sunday the Grindalls drove across the valley in the open Land Rover with Chief ole Moiko and two of his wives, the women sitting on either side of their husband in the rear seat. Rounding a turn, the party was held up by a herd of giraffe crossing the road. Denny, who loved the graceful Maasai giraffe above all Kenya's wild creatures, exclaimed in his feeble Maa about their beauty, their magnificent height, their long, lovely eyelashes and their other marvelous attributes. The chief was amused by this enthusiastic outburst over what he considered a matter of no great importance. Turning to one of his wives, he said, "When I speak with Denny and Jeanne, it is like talking to two little children."

Work was progressing nicely at Pulei Village. The Grindalls had selected a site for their own dwelling, to be occupied at some future date, and construction was under way. The men were put to work laying a drain field and septic tank for the bathhouse in the middle of the compound. Soon there were shower stalls, washbasins with mirrors (a major shock to people who had never seen their own reflections) and even flush toilets. The toilets generated a great deal of discussion and speculation as to their purpose. Their shining whiteness was admired; the float mechanisms were inspected; the seats and covers were touched gingerly. As the plumbing proceeded and the reservoirs were allowed to fill, there were many questions. "How does the water get in there?" "What do we do with it?" "Is it good for us?" "How does it work?"

When Denny flushed one of the toilets experimentally, there was an immediate outburst of astonishment. Denny and Jeanne looked at each other in gradually dawning comprehension. Until this moment it had not occurred to them that they would now have to potty train 150 Maasai men, women and children.

Ten
CRISIS IN KENYA
1974

Early in 1974, while Denny and Jeanne were making church appearances around the cited states and arranging their forthcoming half-year stint in Maasailand, two devastating messages arrived from Kenya. The first was a letter from Colin Crabbee advising them that he had reason to believe the African Church would not renew its invitation to them. The second was a confirming letter from the African Church office in Nairobi.

Denny and Jeanne were deeply hurt but not completely taken by surprise. They remembered the many excuses and delays they had encountered the previous year when they had applied for their 1974 re-entry permit, an absolute requirement for foreigners working in Kenya. Their application had to be endorsed by the African Church to be considered by the Kenyan immigration authorit ies. It was only by persistent prodding that they had finally received the endorsement. Anticipating problems of a more serious nature, Denny had taken pains to contact the friendly government engineer who had visited the Chamness Lake project. From that individual he had received assurances of government support. Based on those assurances and on a good deal of prayer, Denny and Jeanne proceeded with their preparations, not without misgivings.

In the Nairobi headquarters of the African Church, Adam Matadi burst into the office of his superior without waiting to be admitted. A look of consternation creased his broad face. "He's back!" he gasped.

Joseph Kariuki looked up from the papers on his desk and frowned in annoyance. "Who is back? What are you talking about?"

"Grindall! The American! He has returned!"

"Impossible!" snorted the senior official. "You must be mistaken! He has no place to stay, no authority, no sponsorship! How could he be here?"

"I don't know, but he is here, I tell you! I have seen him myself!"

Denny and Jeanne moved directly into their new Maasai house in Pulei Village. Their neighbors were overjoyed to welcome them into the community but also somewhat astounded, for no Whites had ever lived in a Maasai village. Denny built shelving and put up curtains. A small stove fueled by liquid gas served for cooking and occasional heating. A kerosene lantern suspended from a hook in the ceiling provided illumination. Three chairs and a small table constituted the remaining furnishings. They were cozy, comfortable and quite happy in their snug concrete house.

Denny plunged at once into his planned projects. He intended to expand the shamba to a full ten acres, complete the model village and raise the level of Chamness Lake. He planned to increase the lake's capacity and ensure a lasting water supply in the event of a prolonged drought. There would be plenty of other things to do as well: repairing and maintaining the pipeline, finishing the Saikeri dam and responding to requests from other communities, should there be any.

Jeanne's agenda was less defined. She planned to continue teaching her classes, but she worried that time might hang heavy on her hands now that she no longer had the office, clinic and other mission duties to keep her busy. She soon discovered there was no cause for such concern. Each day, from morning to night, the women clustered about her door, curious at first to see how her house was furnished and, later, demanding every conceivable form of assistance. From the first day she was kept so busy that she had to forego keeping up her diary.

The requests of the villagers varied widely in nature, although medical problems far outweighed all others. The medical cases they saw were appalling, most needing professional care far beyond what they were prepared to dispense from their modest first aid satchel, but the people were violently opposed to being taken to a doctor, even when they were offered transportation and financial assistance. Only when the condition became indisputably life-threatening would they consent to be taken to a hospital in Nairobi, for they were convinced that the hospital was a place of death.

Despite the innumerable injuries and ailments, the people had no professional medical assistance available in the district except at Olooseos, and that facility was chronically overtaxed. Some took their complaints to the medicine man, the same *ol-iburi* whose glowering hostility Denny had experienced at his meeting with the district elders. Although there were nearly as many deaths as recoveries following his ministrations, this man wielded considerable power over the people's minds, and he guarded this power jealously.

When patients were brought to him, he would spread his magic sticks on the hide of a spotted calf and mutter strange incantations as he fingered the worn bits of wood. As many came to him out of fear of offending him by seeking other treatment as came to him in expectation of a cure. More and more, the people of Pulei Village came to rely on the Grindalls for medical assistance.

One day a young boy was brought to them with a spear through his leg. It was obvious at once that he was a casualty of one of the boys' war games. The cause of the injury was not the formidable steel-tipped, broad-blade spear of the morans but only a sharpened sapling. With the entire village looking on, the poor lad suffered more acutely from embarrassment than from physical pain. Denny drew the stick out, cleansed the wound with peroxide, smeared Bag Balm on the two openings and wrapped the boy's leg with a bandage.

The villagers watched this operation with interest. At its conclusion one of the elders said, "You know, it's always best to bring these cases to Denny. He has more good medicine than they have at the hospital."

Dental problems were especially difficult. Because of the high milk content in their diet, the people generally possessed strong teeth, though the incisors tended to protrude due to the unusually long-term nursing of infants; however, the total absence of dental hygiene resulted in much decay. With the washroom now in operation it was possible to introduce tooth brushing, but that was of scant comfort to those suffering severe toothaches.

Extraction was the only help the Grindalls were equipped to provide. In any case, the decay was usually so advanced that the infected tooth could not have been salvaged even by a professional dentist. Denny rummaged through his toolbox and found a small pair of vise-grip pliers that proved, if not ideal, at least adequate for most extractions. He was grateful for Maasai stoicism as he adjusted and locked the pliers while diverting his patient's attention with his never-failing banter; then with a brisk yank he drew out the offending tooth, usually before the patient realized what had happened. Recalling these experiences, he says, "I'm glad our dentist son, Steve, wasn't around to watch. He would have had my license lifted for malpractice."

There were opportunities now such as the Grindalls had not enjoyed earlier to observe the fascinating wildlife of East Africa in a natural setting. Each morning they awakened to the joyous medley of thousands of birds, all seemingly intent on outdoing their neighbors in celebrating the explosive African dawn. The small weavers built their nests suspended from tree branches instead of lodging them in the boughs as other birds do. A large acacia might have fifty or more weaver nests hanging like Christmas ornaments from its lower limbs. The starlings, in contrast to their drab American cousins, were feathered in gorgeous iridescent blue, set off by bright golden eyes ringed with a thin circle of white. They congregated at the Grindalls' doorstep each day to beg for crumbs.

There were larger birds too: the heavy-boned Kori bustards, subject of ancient Maasai legends; vultures soaring ceaselessly against the blue sky, their long red necks swinging from side to side as they scanned the plains for carrion; and ostriches stalking sedately through the tall lion grass, the majestic black males ever on the lookout for Maasai warriors, who coveted their ornate plumage.

The most prevalent members of the cat family in that area were the leopards, though lions also made appearances from time to time. Lions, they learned, were more sensitive to the presence of Maasai warriors than to other humans or animals. The males had a healthy fear of the morans. They seemed to know that any apprentice warrior would willingly risk his life for the honor of wearing the headdress that would distinguish him as a lion slayer. Most fascinating of all the animals were the elephants. They moved across the landscape almost soundlessly and with deceptive speed, the young ones running to keep up with the lumbering adults. Their thick, dusty hides, cracked and dried by the sun, itched so unbearably that they were constantly on the alert for a suitable object on which to scratch. Whenever the Grindalls came upon a broken tree, they were sure that some old bull had used it as a scratching post. One day Denny watched a big male elephant back up to one of the massive boulders that are common throughout the Rift Valley. Grabbing his camera, he recorded a series of actions that make up one of the most hilarious segments of the Grindalls' slide show. Working blindly, the old bull couldn't manage to position his itch in exact juxtaposition to the rock. Repeatedly, thinking he had found it, he would lower his great body and rub savagely, but soon he would stop and with seeming vexation, shift another part of his anatomy over the rock. After a half dozen unsuccessful tries he finally brought the rock and the itch together, and the resulting slide, one of the classics in the collection, depicts pachyderm gratification so sensual that it never fails to produce a howl of mirth from the audience.

There were, of course, some hazards associated with living so close to wild animals . . . hazards that were sometimes frightening to the newcomers but commonplace to the villagers. One night they were awakened by a fearful racket coming from the "old village," the original *engang*, which lay several hundred yards away and was still occupied by a few of Simeon's people. In the morning they learned that a leopard had broken through the thornbrush enclosure and killed many sheep and goats before the men were able to drive it away. As soon as daylight came, a pursuit was formed. With uncanny skill, the men tracked the leopard for several miles and finally found it sleeping in a tree, where they killed it with their spears.

On another occasion a lion broke into another *engang* nearby and mauled two men so savagely that both died of their wounds. These courageous men had not hesitated to attack the lion in defense of their livestock, yet none of the Maasai considered it out of the ordinary that their valor had cost them their lives.

An unexpected helper arrived one day: a well-dressed Black man named Jacob Kimaru. The Grindalls had met him a year ago at Kajiado. He was the same scholar who had been commissioned by the Bible Society to translate the New Testament into Maa. He spoke earnestly of the need to bring to his Maasai people the good news of Christ in written form. He said, "I have seen what you and Reverend Pulei are doing here, and I would like very much to join you while I complete my work."

Denny and Jeanne were impressed by the scholar's earnestness. They felt privileged to support such a worthwhile project. They brought him under the care of MASI and placed him on the payroll. Denny built and furnished a ferro-cement house somewhat larger than the standard concrete dwelling to accommodate his work and put a vehicle at his disposal.

They would have been well advised to look more carefully into this man's background before granting him their complete trust.

Seven years earlier, the Bible Society had received a similar proposal from Kimaru. They had also responded enthusiastically by commissioning him to carry out his work under the society's sponsorship. They, too, were thrilled by the opportunity to bring Christianity to the Maasai people, but when, at the end of three years, they inquired into the translator's progress, they were distressed to discover that nothing had been accomplished. When after four more years he had not completed the translation of even one whole book, they gave up and withdrew their sponsorship. The Grindalls learned of this only after they, too, became disillusioned.

In early 1975, while Denny and Jeanne were in the United States, a letter from Samuel aroused their first misgivings concerning Jacob Kimaru. Samuel reported that the translator was inviting distinguished visitors to the model village and representing himself as the person responsible for what was being accomplished there. This came at a time when Kimaru had been at Pulei Village only a few months! To reinforce his air of authority, he lorded it over Samuel in the visitors' presence, giving the impression that Pulei was a workman under Kimaru's direction.

Another communication came a month before the Grindalls' return to Kenya, causing even greater misgivings. Samuel reported intercepting a carelessly sealed letter to Kimaru from Barclay's Bank in Nairobi. Already suspicious, Samuel opened the envelope and discovered a bank receipt for the equivalent of ten thousand dollars! Denny was on full alert when he and Jeanne arrived in Kenya in June 1975, and at the earliest opportunity he put the matter squarely before Kimaru.

"Jacob, I understand you have a bank account. Is that right?" For the first time, the translator seemed ill at ease. He acknowledged that a major Christian organization had given him "a little bit of money" to use in helping them gain access to the Maasai people. Denny saw this as a clear conflict of interest and insisted that Kimaru either return the money and accept no more financial assistance from this other organization or leave MASI employment. Kimaru agreed to "think it over" and after a few days informed Denny that he had decided to leave and devote himself wholly to his new sponsor's work. He departed with his sizeable bank account.

Denny later confronted the regional director of Kimaru's new sponsor and expressed his resentment for what had been done. This man explained somewhat feebly that Kimaru's "worldwide fame as a member of the Maasai royal family" had brought him to their attention as one who could help them work with the Maasai. Denny's further protests brought only a lame expression of regret from the American headquarters office.

Jacob Kimaru is now a rich man. He is known throughout Kenya as an influential contact with the Maasai tribe and is well rewarded by his employers. Unfortunately, however, he is not a member of the (nonexistent) Maasai royal family or even a true member of the tribe but actually a Kikuyu by birth who has learned and found ways to ingratiate himself with his adopted fellow tribesmen. When Denny Grindall meets him on the streets of Nairobi, the distinguished scholar's normally proud demeanor reflects acute embarrassment.

These were busy days. Women came even from outside the district to attend Jeanne's classes, some from more than twenty miles away. Growing numbers of villagers were requesting houses "of latest American design." Denny built a playground for the children, who nearly wore out the slide, swings and teeter-totter in their enthusiasm. The shamba was producing such fabulous crops that a vegetable stand had to be built to market the surplus. Chief Simeon, revealing a shrewd instinct for business, installed a trading post where the people could buy small tools, utensils, needles, thread and similar necessities. Meanwhile, preparations were being made to raise the dam on Chamness Lake.

Samuel Pulei was now involved in all the developmental work launched by the Grindalls as well as in overseeing the dozen or so young Maasai evangelists who served the area. Contact with his superiors had become minimal; there was, in fact, an ominous silence from that direction, but he was so busy and so pleased to be doing what he had always considered his life's work that he scarcely noticed. Denny and Jeanne were equally preoccupied.

Then, like a clap of thunder that presages an unexpected summer storm, an official letter was delivered to Denny by a government messenger. It ordered him to appear on a designated date before the district commissioner at Kajiado to answer certain unspecified charges.

Denny's normally cheerful countenance clouded with apprehension as he read the brief, curt letter aloud to Jeanne. "This is it, honey," he said gloomily. "Now I know how Daniel felt when he was thrown to the lions."

"What do you think it means?" she asked.

"They're kicking us out of the country. I should have seen it coming."

"What makes you so sure?" Jeanne asked.

"It has all the signs. If a foreigner gets on the wrong side of a citizen and a complaint is made, they just expel the troublemaker."

She took his hand quietly in her own. "Well, I'm not so sure of that. It seems to me that if the Lord brought us here he's not going to let us be thrown out before we finish his work. Why don't we ask him now for protection?"

As they prayed, the wonderful "peace that passes understanding" settled upon them. Calmly, they continued in their planned activities as if nothing troubling had occurred.

At the scheduled date and time, Denny drove to Kajiado and found the office of the district commissioner. Inside he discovered Joseph Kariuki and Adam Matadi hunched nervously in a small reception room. A cool exchange of greetings was followed by a gloomy silence. After an uncomfortably long wait the three men were summoned before the district commissioner.

Commissioner Karui was a big man, imposingly official in his well-tailored khaki uniform. On the polished mahogany desk before him was a pith helmet of the style introduced by the early British settlers. Other accoutrements, the somber paneling and the enormous notarial seal with its curving handle, gave evidence of the imperial influence. The commissioner motioned for the visitors to be seated as he rifled through some papers. At length he turned to the two churchmen. "Well, gentlemen," he said briskly, "I read your representations. I believe I understand the problem. Have you anything to add?"

Joseph Kariuki spoke stiffly, his voice taut with nervousness. "We wish to make your honor aware that this man, Denny Grindall, and his wife have been engaging in unauthorized activities among the Maasai people. They were admitted several years ago under the sponsorship of the African Church, which we represent, but since that time they have not accepted all the conditions required for them to continue their activities here under our sponsorship."

"What are those conditions?" the district commissioner inquired mildly.

Kariuki was beginning to perspire. "Well, your honor, there were ten conditions in all, but the principal ones were that foreign financial donations intended for activities to be conducted here under our sponsorship must be turned over to the African Church, and that such funds must be used exclusively for purposes designated by the African Church."

At this point, Denny expected the interrogation to switch to himself. Instead, the commissioner continued to address the two clergymen. His tone and manner now changed noticeably. From the detached inquirer after facts, he suddenly became a mild-mannered judge offering fatherly advice to a couple of juvenile offenders.

"Let me tell you, gentlemen, that I know exactly what the Grindalls are doing here. I also learned last year that you did not want to help them renew their visas. I can tell you now that the Republic of Kenya is prepared to issue the Grindalls a ten-year unconditional work permit and to offer them whatever assistance they need. If the

African Church does not want them here, this government wants them, because we believe that what they are doing is exactly what needs to be done."

A stunned silence followed. Commissioner Karui leaned back in his swivel chair and regarded the two accusers with a benign gaze. "Now, is there anything else we need to discuss?" he inquired gently. There was no response. The commissioner rose, smiling. "I believe that will be all then. Thank you for coming in, gentlemen, and good day."

Eleven
BLESSINGS FROM THE LORD
1975-1983

After five arduous years, the Grindalls' venture at last seemed reasonably secure. Despite the continuing animosity of the African Church, which was a great burden on their spirits (Jeanne's diary notes sadly, "It is quite distressing to have ministers hate you"), they now had the government of Kenya solidly behind them. In the United States, and even in other parts of the world, their work was beginning to be recognized.

TIME magazine carried a laudatory piece; later *Reader's Digest* printed an article entitled "Miracle of the Maasai," and other publications also picked up the story. As a result of this publicity, coupled with their appearances at many churches throughout the United States, MASI was on firm financial footing. Then, while they were out of the country, another crisis occurred in Kenya.

In April, near the third anniversary of the deluge that filled Chamness Lake overnight, another emptied it as speedily. This time it was a colossal torrent of rain, a monsoon that swept in from the Indian Ocean bringing an inundation of such magnitude as might occur only once in two or three decades. Highways and concrete bridges that had withstood the onslaught of nature for years simply vanished, while the gullies and wadis roared with water.. Chamness Lake filled to its brim, then the mighty river shooting over its spillway began to erode its earthen wall. Slowly at first, then with increasing rapidity, the rocks that held the earth in place began to yield. Finally, with a grinding roar, the entire east end of the dam gave way and the contents of the lake belched out across the plain.

Upon arriving according to their custom in mid-June, the Grindalls surveyed the damage. The scene was anything but encouraging. Beyond a gaping hole forty or fifty feet across in the east end of the dam a new river bed had been carved. The rocks that Denny's crew had collected so laboriously and carried in their arms to the work site were scattered for a quarter of a mile or more downstream. The lake bed was empty except for a few stagnant pools, and even those were nearly inaccessible because of the muddy lake floor.

Samuel was watching Denny's face intently. "What shall we do now?" he asked anxiously.

Denny flashed his indomitable grin. "Why, we'll fix it, Sam. And this time we'll fix it so it will stay fixed."

He concluded that the spillway width had been too narrow for the extraordinary flow and the structure not solid enough to resist the turbulence of the flood. His design had been adequate for normal conditions, but it had not withstood the extreme stress. All his working life he had been obliged to learn by trial and error; this was just another instance where error provided a valuable lesson.

The men of Olosho-Oibor took heart when they saw how quickly Simba recovered his spirits. They cheerfully set to work under his supervision to repair the dam. He made the spillway three times as wide and reinforced it with many additional tons of rock and concrete against the rolling turbulence that would accompany another major flood. At this writing, no further damage has been experienced.

One who did not rejoice in the repair of the dam was the *ol-iburi*. Day after day while the work was in progress, he sat sphinxlike on a nearby promontory, his thick legs crossed and his arms folded, staring fixedly at the activity. Sometimes other elders came and sat with him. There was never evidence of communication within this group; the men simply sat and watched. One day Denny casually remarked that he was going to invite these idlers to join in the work. Jonah shook his head emphatically.

"No, Simba. Ol-iburi not work. He say what you do is bad for Maasai."

With a shrug, Denny returned to his labor, wondering as he did so whether the medicine man was actually trying to sabotage the reservoir through his occult art.

From his earliest projects, Denny had grappled with a problem even more challenging than the collection of water: how to make the water more accessible. Aside from the pipeline running down from the hillside and supplying Pulei Village by gravity, his other projects, Chamness and Saikeri, still required hand-carrying of water to the villages. Pipelines could be laid from the reservoirs to the villages. Since by their nature as well as by design, though, these reservoirs were situated in the lowest-lying areas in the vicinity, pumps would be needed to raise the water and deliver it over great distances to its users. But without electricity, how were the pumps to be driven?

The obvious answer was the Rift Valley wind, which blew strong and steady throughout the year. From the moment of his decision to build the dam, Denny had kept windmills in mind, but he soon learned that windmills of the size he wanted would cost about $4500 apiece and require very precise installation. Also, there was hazard involved in placing heavy machinery on tiny platforms thirty or forty feet in the air. Now, thanks to the generosity of MASI's supporters, cost was no longer an obstacle, and after five years of experience his Maasai crew, under careful direction, could handle the work. During one of their speaking tours in the Midwest, the Grindalls visited the Dempster Mills in Beatrice, Nebraska, the only surviving major windmill manufacturer in America. They acquainted the managers with their work in Maasailand. Dempster offered full support at wholesale prices and loaded Denny with installation instructions. The Upper Darby church underwrote the cost of one windmill, the La Canada church in California another, and other groups contributed sizeable sums toward the purchase of two more.

Positioning the windmills correctly in relation to the reservoir was critical. A large conduit of rectangular shape (a hooded spillway) was buried in the dam. A manually controlled gate regulated the lake level by spilling water into a series of storage ponds, which had been created at the time of the dam's construction. Their depth, location and spacing were based on the ultimate purpose of each pond, which was to supply enough water to keep one windmill pumping.

The Dempster specifications called for anchoring each leg of the tower in concrete. The four legs were to be joined, thirty-eight feet above the pond level, to support a wooden platform four feet square. On this platform would rest the gear box that was to transmit the wind's power from the revolving vanes to the storage pond below.

The assembly sequence was extremely critical. The slightest deviation was certain to result in confusion and frustration. Denny was putting the platform in place on the first tower just as Jeanne arrived with some visitors; then he discovered that he had left the assembly instructions behind. To the amusement of the visitors, he was obliged to lower a bucket for the instructions.

Next came the most hazardous step: hoisting the 475-pound gear box onto the tower. In Seattle, Denny had made nylon safety belts, and with these he secured several men at intermediate levels on the tower to help raise the gear box. Slowly and painstakingly, the task proceeded until the heavy mechanism came up over the edge of the platform and was positioned precisely for alignment with the drive rod that would actuate the pump below. Next the great vanes were attached. Slowly at first, they began to turn.

Eyes glistening, young George Sekuda expressed the excitement of all the Maasai in the best English he could command. "That wind machine is just ridiculous."

For the first time anywhere in the Rift Valley, water was delivered by nature's power to a Maasai village.

Over the years, four more windmills were installed, and a pipeline was extended through the valley of Olosho-Oibor, with a spur line running out to each village along the way. With these increasing demands on the big reservoir and the 18,000 gallons of reserve supply in the tanks at Pulei Village, Denny began considering ways to reduce waste. The windmills were already working as hard as they could. He put in four ram pumps powered by gravity flow from the dam, and by this means was able to eliminate water loss.

The success of the windmills produced an unexpected result: the abrupt departure of Denny's old nemesis, the *ol-iburi*.

"Him go 'way," Jonah reported with satisfaction. "Say him medicine no more *sedah* (good)."

However, the joy of the latest achievement was somewhat dimmed by new problems with the African Church. The Kenya government's official sponsorship of MASI had angered them. Samuel received a letter ordering him to appear before a church court after first submitting a written admission of wrongful action against his superiors. This he refused to do, saying "I am not convinced that what I have done is wrong." The response was that he must then appear before a church disciplinary board. The meeting, ostensibly inspired by Samuel's alleged attempts to "break the church," was stormy and inconclusive. Clearly intended to shake his composure, it only strengthened his resolve to continue the work he was doing. He answered the charges and questions vigorously and with considerable heat. At last the badgering ended with a vague directive that Samuel could continue with his MASI activity but must report anything he observed that would "benefit the church in any way." Indignantly he said, "What? I don't understand that." No explanation was offered. He returned to Olosho-Oibor sorely vexed.

As he reflected unhappily on the incident, Samuel was convinced he had not heard the last of the matter. The next move, he felt certain, would be his transfer to another post. He did not have long to wait. A letter arrived assigning him to the position of superintendent of church schools in the Nairobi area. Realizing that refusal of the assignment would cost him his certificate as a pastor and therefore diminish rather than enhance his ability to serve his people, he reluctantly accepted. At the same time, he raised a practical question. Since he did not own a car, how could he perform duties that would require so much travel? His superiors assured him that they would lend him money with which to purchase a car, but the loan was never made.

Samuel's reassignment was a severe blow to the Grindalls. They had come to depend heavily on his knowledge, his influence on the Maasai people and, most of all, on his services as translator. They recognized, of course, that this blow was aimed at themselves in retaliation for the African Church's humiliating defeat at the hands of the district commissioner. They also realized that this animosity grew out of envy, for in the church officials' eyes, all the acclaim heaped on the Grindalls, as well as the financial support they were receiving, properly belonged to the African Church.

Samuel struggled for a year in his new assignment, but his heart was not in it. Sadly, he tendered his resignation. In his letter he stated bluntly that he could no longer work with his hands tied. He wanted only to be free to work with his beloved people. If he could no longer officially be a man of God, he would simply be God's man, doing what he knew God wanted him to do.

His superiors reacted with alarm. "Oh, sorry. You should not resign. We do not have another Maasai contact. There is only you. If you resign it will be very bad for your people!"

Samuel's long-smoldering anger burst forth in a flood of bitter words. "Why are you battering and torturing me? You do not listen to my advice. You don't care about the Maasai people; you only want to take pictures of them so you can raise money in America and England. You are making a museum of Maasailand! I am annoyed with you! Let me go! I can no longer bear your church politics. I have to go!"

After this, from time to time an emissary from the Church came to Samuel and begged him to return to the fold. His only response was silence.

The one who eventually broke the deadlock was the Reverend Bernard Muindi, a Meru, who was at the time second only to Joseph Kariuki in the hierarchy of the African Church. Muindi, a clear-thinking, steady man and himself a victim of persecution by church politicians, had somehow retained his zeal while learning by painful experience to work within the system. He wrote a gentle personal letter to Samuel, the essence of which was as follows:

Samuel, the church has decided to assign you to the work of Denny Grindall. You work with him and nobody will bother you any longer. If you accept this, write us a letter and say you agree. Samuel's reply was a model of brevity: "Yes, I agree."

This action permitted Denny to place Samuel on MASI's payroll, where he remained until his retirement in December 1989. The move clearly indicated that the church officials had grown weary of the long battle. Throughout the tension the Grindalls consistently credited the African Church with sponsorship of their many projects. In every way, they sought to bring about not merely a truce but a genuine reconciliation. Several years passed before these gestures were acknowledged; then one day the entire ten-man board of directors of the Maasai Rural Development Center came to call on the Grindalls. The delegation admitted that the African Church had made a grave mistake in trying to have the two Americans expelled from the country. They said humbly, "We want you to come back under our sponsorship so we can really be part of your work." Jeanne and Denny rejoiced in this answer to their many prayers. Today, MASI and the African Church share a warm and mutually trusting relationship.

As the years passed, more dams were built . . . seven in all. Rich as were the benefits, these manmade ponds and lakes also created some hazards. Malaria is a scourge in the wetter parts of East Africa, and with the coming of these sizeable reservoirs, mosquitoes were beginning to appear for the first time in the valley of Olosho-Oibor. Also, there was some degradation of water quality, especially after long periods of drought, due to the growth of algae. Denny pondered these two problems and hit upon a single environmentally sound solution.

He learned that a species of tropical fish called *Talapia* did well in artificial enclosures and were available from a hatchery north of

Nairobi. These fish, resembling crappie or sunfish, had excellent survival characteristics and could be obtained in several varieties, some feeding on mosquito larvae and some on algae. Denny purchased several thousand fingerlings of each variety and transported them in plastic bags to Chamness Lake. The people of the nearby villages, who had never seen or even heard of fish, were immensely interested in this experiment. Many spectators pressed close around Denny as he opened the bags and began pouring the fingerlings into the lake. Playfully, he handed a minnow to a young girl. She accepted it automatically, then dropped it with a shriek when it wriggled in her hand.

"Why, you shouldn't be afraid of that harmless little fellow," Denny chided her. "Some day when he grows big you'll have him for dinner."

"Ugh," the girl exclaimed with a shudder. "I could never eat that wiggly, slimy thing! I'd rather eat a snake."

"And yet," Denny laughs as he recalls the incident, "she could go home and have a bowl of sour milk mixed with cow's blood and think it was delicious. It's all a matter of culture."

The talapia flourished and multiplied, growing eventually to about twelve inches and something over a pound in weight. Although the flesh is excellent, with a texture arid flavor much like halibut, the Maasai have yet to overcome their aversion to the thought of eating fish.

Denny also introduced black bass and a species of Japanese carp, and these too did well. As the population grew in the original planting site, he moved them in tanks on his truck to other reservoirs, so that eventually all the dams were well stocked. The water quality improved markedly, and malaria did not gain a foothold in the district.

When, after a long drought, one of the smaller reservoirs appeared in danger of drying up, Denny decided to move its entire fish population to a larger dam to ensure against their loss. The water in the threatened pond being at this point only waist deep, he organized a party of men equipped with a length of chicken-wire fencing, which they stretched like a seine as they waded slowly in a moving line from one end of the reservoir to the other. The trapped fish were mature black bass, some well over ten pounds. As they began to concentrate at the end of the pond, their activity grew increasingly violent. While some of the men held the net in place to prevent escape, Denny had others wade among the thrashing, flopping fish to capture them in their hands and transfer them to a tank of water on the back of his truck. Once in the confines of the tank, the fish unaccountably stopped thrashing about and remained motionless.

It was a scene of hilarious confusion. The men doing the capturing grappled with the lively bass as nervously as if they were cornering crocodiles while the others, safe behind the wire seine, roared with laughter. Finally all the fish were safely caught and placed in the tank. Denny, with David ole Kisera as his helper, drove to a larger reservoir.

Young David was puzzled by the sudden submissiveness of the captured fish. "What makes them so busy in the pond," he asked, "and so polite when they get in the tank?"

Solomon wrote, "Where there is no vision, the people perish" (Prov 29:18 KJV). How aptly his words apply to the Maasai people. At Olosho-Oibor, where the magnificent vision of Samuel, Simeon and Lainkini inspired their fellow clansmen, great wonders were achieved. In other communities, though, where vision was lacking, progress came slowly if at all. Ewaso was a case in point.

In 1976 Denny built a large earth reservoir near the village of Ewaso. The following year he constructed a smaller one across the road from the first, lining it with butyl rubber to prevent seepage. The villagers, although pleased, offered no thanks, for Maasai pride discourages the recipient of a gift from expressing gratitude. Nevertheless, they begged another favor. Would Denny also build them a school so their children could enjoy the benefits of education like the children of Pulei Village? Denny agreed and set a date to join the Ewaso volunteers and commence construction.

He was enthusiastic about the project for a couple of reasons. This request, coming from the people of the community, was an encouraging indication that at least some Maasai were overcoming the traditional tribal distrust of education. Increasingly, the Kenya government was urging each family to send at least one child to school; however, the Maasai usually complied grudgingly, if at all, by sending only crippled or feeble-minded children who could not tend goats and sheep. For the people of Ewaso actually to request a school was a good sign of changing attitudes. Also, this project would give Denny a chance to use the beautiful local stone, which appeared ideal for construction.

His enthusiasm suffered a rude jolt, however, when he and Samuel arrived at the site at the appointed time and found no volunteers present. After a reasonable wait they departed, thinking there could have been some confusion about the date. They returned next day but still found no one. Perplexed and disappointed, Denny turned to Samuel for an explanation. Samuel was deeply mortified; it was characteristic of him to assume personal responsibility for any failure by his people. "It is just the way of the Maasai," he said unhappily.

"But why would they ask for a school if they weren't serious?" Denny demanded.

Samuel looked uncomfortable. "I think they wanted it because we have one, but they don't want it enough to work for it."

Ordinarily, that would have been the end of the matter, for Denny usually insisted that the beneficiaries of a project share in its labor and cost; otherwise, there would be no project. This time, however, he decided to make an exception.

"Well, they asked for a school, and they're going to get one. Maybe a little healthy shame will be good for them."

He organized a crew of six or seven evangelists and several Olo-sho-Oibor volunteers. With the help of these people, he built a schoolhouse and, for added measure, a church, both of native stone. Today both are thriving. Denny's message appears to have been taken to heart by the elders of Ewaso.

Jeanne's classes continued to attract women from all over the district. Each session started with an hour of hymn singing and Bible study led by Samuel before Jeanne took charge of the program. The classes, which were held in the new *alelacei* under the spreading thorn tree, were marred only by complaints from the local women about flies brought in by outsiders. Remembering that only a couple of years earlier, those who now complained had endured the hordes of flies that swarmed around the old village, Denny and Jeanne were amused by their new fastidiousness.

The dressmaking classes gradually phased out as the women mastered all they cared to learn. Jeanne also dropped knitting instruction when she found that her pupils preferred a mechanical service that was commercially available in the town of Ngong. She began teaching beadwork, which she hoped would grow into a lucrative home industry for the women. She emphasized quality, an alien concept to her pupils. Although for centuries Maasai women had been creating exquisite beadwork for themselves, their children and their warriors, the idea of doing equally fine work for mere "outsiders" held little appeal. Jeanne was aware that other tribes were selling excellent beadwork of their own design in the tourist markets. Realizing that the demand was not unlimited, she looked for a simple article that her pupils could make easily and that she could help sell. The item she finally selected was an ornamental key-ring tab.

To make such an item, she cut a round or oval strip of untanned goatskin and attached it to a split ring of the type commonly used for carrying keys. Decorated with tiny colored beads in a striking Maasai design, this simple object became a fascinating conversation piece. To instill the concept of quality, she appealed to the strong Maasai competitive spirit by making each work session a contest. The five best key rings made each week were displayed for all to examine, and the one who had made the best of the five received a supply of beads.

Marketing the key rings proved easy. Being small and flat, they could be carried in quantity. The Grindalls had no trouble selling them for two dollars apiece at their church appearances in America. The receipts were turned over to Samuel, who then compensated the makers. After some early resistance, the beadwork project turned into a modestly successful enterprise.

These were joy-filled, productive years for the Grindalls. As a result of the magazine articles and the slide presentations around the United States, money was pouring in to their Seattle account, at times accumulating to as much as $75,000 more than needed for the work planned. This enabled them to expand their activities beyond their wildest imaginings. From the six evangelists initially under Samuel's tutelage, the number rose to thirty and then to forty. Another pastor, Samuel Nakeel, was engaged to assist Samuel Pulei. Two more vehicles were added, plus tractors, generators, tools and building materials in ever-increasing quantities. Denny began building dams costing $40,000 or more. MASI was making a contribution that extended well beyond the valley of Olosho-Oibor. Thanks to the faithful MASI volunteers, there were no administrative costs.

In the face of these developments, Denny and Jeanne could only marvel at God's liberality. They were reminded of the words of the prophet Malachi: " '. . . Test me in this,' says the LORD Almighty, 'and see if I will not throw open the floodgates of heaven and pour out so much blessing that you will not have room enough for it' " (Mal 3:10).

Twelve
SAMUEL'S STORY

No people in the world love their children more than do the Maasai. When a Maasai mother sings a lullaby to her baby, she is apt to croon softly the word *engonyakonya*, which in Maa means "grow up, my child." By this she hopes to ward off all the countless hazards that a Maasai child must survive. She also intends to convey her desire that the child will emerge from childhood as a successful adult, fully able to cope with all the challenges of adulthood.

Today, when the world around them is moving inexorably away from their way of life, when survival itself demands adaptation to the hated ways of that outside world, it is harder than ever for a Maasai to "grow up" successfully. Each must find his or her own path.

The path chosen by Samuel Pulei was unlike that of any of his fellow tribesmen. It led him to become one of the first of his people to be truly educated and one of the very first to be ordained as a Christian pastor.

Samuel's miraculous survival as an infant was told in the opening chapter of this book. His youthful rebellion and self-imposed exile, which in his rigidly controlled Maasai culture were nearly as remarkable as his earlier escape from a grisly death, have also been described. By all the laws of probability, his fragile infant life should have been extinguished at its beginning. When, by some remote chance, he miraculously escaped that seemingly certain fate, there still seemed not to be the slimmest possibility of his ever achieving a more notable career than that of a herdsman of goats and cattle. But the God who made Ntienput Pulei cares nothing for probabilities, denies the existence of chance and laughs at foolish human predictions of a man's destiny.

Following Ntienput's flight from his stricken village came a period of hardship, loneliness, gradual self-discovery and slow, painful struggle toward a seemingly impossible goal. If ever a human being was fired in the crucible of adversity, if ever a youth followed unswervingly a vision against crushing opposition and over insurmountable obstacles, it was this quiet Maasai herd boy.

When the young Ntienput enrolled in the Ololua Primary School, he had to learn English in order to follow the instruction. He also needed to work at whatever tasks he could find to support himself and pay his tuition. However, he had the biological advantage of being older than his classmates and the motivational edge of being in a greater hurry to learn. Ntienput's instructors quickly recognized that he was "clever," as the English quaintly put it, and started him in the third grade instead of the first. His progress through primary school and high school was greatly accelerated, as he easily passed all his examinations. During his early school years, he became a Christian and took the biblical name of Samuel.

Samuel graduated from high school in 1958 at the age of twenty-four. (This is an estimate. Like many African births, his was not recorded.) For a time he thought of becoming a doctor, but the cost of a medical education put that goal far beyond his reach. After returning to his village for a short stay, he became an "untrained teacher" at his old primary school at Ololua. Later he served first as a certified teacher and then headmaster of that same school. It was at Ololua during this period that his encounter with Joseph Kariuka led to his seminary instruction and subsequent ordination.

Until he was nearly forty, Samuel knew only a life of grinding poverty. When as a seminary student he met and married Edith, they were, as John Bunyan wrote much earlier of himself and his bride, "without so much household stuff as a dish or a spoon." Even his assignment to the Moranga parish as a commissioned church worker and his later ordination as pastor to that parish did little to relieve the situation. His salary was pitifully small. Then, following his year of instruction in England and reassignment to Olooseos, his stipend was mysteriously cut off altogether, leaving him totally without income for most of a year. The explanation for this catastrophe, which he learned only some time later, was that a dispute had arisen between the Ngong parish and the headquarters of the African Church at Nairobi over which of them should pay his salary. While the issue was being resolved, neither paid him.

During the early years of Samuel's ministry, the family's living conditions were little better than those of his relatives still dwelling in mud-and-dung huts. Samuel owned a small piece of ground near Olooseos. On it was a decrepit three-room frame house with a single door, no windows other than square holes covered by sagging shutters, and an earthen floor. In this wretched hovel, so ravaged by termites that one could shove a stick through any of its four walls, Edith raised her growing brood. Samuel helped only when he was able to obtain leave from his parish duties.

One day, not long after Samuel's return from England, he and Edith went to visit her family in their small home outside Nairobi. While they were there Edith's younger sister, a schoolgirl in her early teens, became desperately ill. Samuel and Edith were naturally concerned, but their questions drew only vague and evasive responses. The girl's condition worsened alarmingly; soon it became apparent that she was in labor. Samuel and Edith rushed her to a nearby hospital only an hour before she delivered. The baby was a girl, perfect in every way, but neither her mother nor her grandparents demonstrated joy in her birth. The grandparents declared that the infant would have to be "thrown away," and even the mother insisted that she did not want to keep it.

"Oh, no," Samuel protested, "you must not let anything happen to her. We will come back in a week to help you with your problem."

Samuel and Edith returned in a week as promised, although they had not fully resolved the matter between themselves. "We don't have milk for our own children," Edith lamented, for this was during the time when Samuel's salary had been discontinued. But Samuel was immovable. They asked Edith's sister if she intended to keep her baby. She shook her head, saying only that she wanted to go back to school. Her parents were more determined than ever to throw the baby away. Samuel, who may have been thinking of his own crisis in infancy, said, "We will take her and raise her ourselves."

On the way home Edith tearfully repeated that they were without means to care decently for their own children; how could they possibly feed another mouth?

Keeping his eyes fixed on the road ahead, Samuel said doggedly,

"The Lord will provide. I know that he will."

The Grindalls were by then working with Samuel and beginning to gain some insight into his financial circumstances, though not through any hint from him. Soon they found ways to provide occasional assistance to the family. When the little girl, whom the new parents had named Nicea, was about three, Samuel introduced her to the Grindalls, saying, "These are the people who gave you milk when you were a baby. Without them, you would not have had enough to eat."

Nicea is now a beautiful, well-adjusted teen-ager. Not long ago, she came to Samuel in tears, saying that she had overheard some people talking about her. They said that Samuel and Edith were not her real parents.

Gently, Samuel told her as much of the story as he felt she could handle. Drying her eyes, she said, "I wish I hadn't heard those people talking, but I don't care. You *are* my real parents."

Samuel, Denny and some of Samuel's Maasai friends built the Puleis a concrete house "of latest American design." MASI paid for the materials. It was three times as large as the compact units at Pulei Village. Samuel battled the eland and impala to develop a shamba, and his poultry business gradually prospered. Eventually he built a fine modern house, a barn and many outbuildings. He planted fruit trees and added sheep and cattle to his holdings. By Maasai standards, he has become modestly prosperous. From time to time, when one of his warrior brothers comes to him looking for something to eat, Samuel sends him away with a pullet (a young hen) and some potatoes and a few words of big-brotherly advice about the benefits of the Christian life.

Some years ago, Endorop moved into a house not far from her son Samuel's farm. She became a Christian but in every other way remains an unreconstructed Maasai, old-fashioned and disdainful of modern ways. Samuel looks in on her frequently and keeps her comfortable and secure.

In all of Maasailand today there is no more venerated and respected native leader than Samuel Pulei. His influence among "the people of the cattle" is unequalled. Paradoxically, however, he is not seen by his fellow tribesmen as a true Maasai, for he is an educated man. His uncle, Senteu, was right when he foretold, more than forty years ago, that Samuel would become a "lost" Maasai if he gave up tribal ways. By doing so, however, he has been able to serve his people more effectively than he ever could have done if he had become a warrior, an elder or even a chief.

"*Engonyakonya:* grow up, my child." Some do; others do not. Perhaps it will always be so.

Thirteen
THE WIND OF CHANGE

In a major speech in Cape Town, South Africa, in 1960, Great Britain's Prime Minister Harold Macmillan said, "The wind of change is blowing through the continent [Africa]. Whether we like it or not, this growth of national consciousness is a political fact. We must accept it as a fact." Within four years most of Britain's colonies south of the Sahara would be independent nations. Africa's "wind of change" began blowing in Kenya in earnest during the 1970s, and would affect the Maasai tribe in a particularly significant way.

Today, a little more than a quarter of a century after independence, it is clear that two major government policies, land demarcation and universal education, are profoundly altering traditional Maasai life.

The Maasai have always been nomadic herdsmen. Today, nomadism is hopelessly obsolete, a reality that has become obvious to everyone except those same nomads who cling fanatically to their precarious way of life. Tea, coffee and sisal plantations, game parks, resorts, highways, airports and new communities, all lie squarely in the historic paths of the wandering herdsmen, cutting them off from the grass and water they must have for their animals. It is the total lack of roots in their tradition that makes nomadism so threatening to Maasai survival. As long as they are constantly moving about, they are cut off from such stabilizing and beneficial resources as schools, health clinics and decent housing.

To the Kenya government, individual land ownership offers the most promising cure for nomadism. Unfortunately, to the Maasai land ownership is an alien notion that makes no sense. Like sunlight, grass and water, land is something that only Engai can own.

Maasailand is an irregular strip of the Great Rift Valley running north and south about seven hundred miles and, at its widest, something over two hundred miles from east to west. It straddles the border separating Kenya from Tanzania, with about two-thirds of its semiarid plain lying to the north of that border. Every Maasai considers himself a co-owner of this vast grassland.

In administering its demarcation policy, the government of Kenya parcels out tracts of formerly unowned territory such as Maasailand to heads of families living nearby. Soon after receiving title to his tract, the Maasai property owner discovers that, even though he does not understand how, he has acquired something other people want. It usually comes about in this way: a Kikuyu neighbor offers him 40,000 or 50,000 shillings for the seemingly worthless piece of paper recently given to him by a government chief. Thinking of the secondhand automobile, motorcycle or of the comely young wife he could buy with such a sum, the Maasai readily agrees to the sale. Later he discovers that he has rendered himself homeless.

Samuel's farm, until recently situated in the midst of his own people, is now completely surrounded by small Kikuyu shambas. He does his best to dissuade the Maasai from giving up their land, but with little success.

School attendance is now strongly encouraged through the primary grades. The policy is not always vigorously administered, and the Maasai, who see little value in educating their children, take advantage of the lax policy. When pressure is applied, the typical Maasai father is apt to respond by sending only one of his children to school, usually the one he values least. This is almost never a girl. The education of girls, after all, is well known to be an outrageous waste; moreover, if a daughter is nearing marriageable age, who but a fool would send her off where she would be certain to escape the notice of a rich Maasai elder wanting to buy a wife? Even today, during school term most school-age girls are found at home in their villages.

Moranhood, once the heart and soul of Maasai tradition, is clearly living out its last days. The warriors' former usefulness to tribal life is no longer valid. Lions and leopards are only seen in the game parks, and the police easily maintain peace between formerly warring tribes. By the end of this century the only morans still to be seen will be those on the payrolls of tourist hotels.

Samuel's evangelist program has succeeded despite many setbacks. Young men with a heart for the Lord are trained to go out into the villages and cattle camps preaching the gospel and encouraging the people to accept Christ. The Maasai, who have always loved drama and mystery, listen with interest and many are converted. Church organization follows, with MASI constructing and equipping each church and fostering its continuing growth. At this writing, sixty-seven churches thrive in Samuel's Maasailand, where twenty years ago there were none.

One who contributed much to the evangelist program was a young American pastor, Tim Fairman, who brought his wife and two small daughters to Pulei Village. He worked with the Grindalls for several seasons. A gifted linguist and teacher, Tim was a great help to Samuel in training the evangelists.

By 1983 Denny Simba Maasai, the "strong young man" of 1970, was in his late sixties. He and Jeanne were beginning to feel the need to rest from their labors. They had accomplished most of what they believed the Lord wanted them to do. From their earliest days in Kenya, they had vowed not to extend their time of service longer than was desired or needed by their Maasai friends. Their constant prayer was that leaders with vision and technicians with ability would emerge among the Maasai people, making their own presence unnecessary. Although this had not come about as fully as they would have liked, they sensed the time for their departure was near. An event in 1983 strengthened this opinion.

The pipeline network, spreading out from Pulei Village, now served all the *engangs* of the valley of Olosho-Oibor, and the immense storage tanks had sufficient capacity to supply still more people with water. All that was needed was to extend the pipeline. Denny made a presentation to the elders of Ngaarov (pronounced "Nahrozh"), a village several miles north of Olosho-Oibor. Knowing that the two-inch steel pipe would be costly, he anticipated resistance. Accordingly, he laid out a conservative plan.

"Maasai," he began, "I know you do not like to sell many of your cattle, so I will ask my Christian friends in America to help with the expense of the project I will propose to you. It is this. Together, we will buy enough pipe this year to bring water one mile closer to your village; then next year another mile and so on until the water is here where we are now. Each year you will have a shorter distance to carry water and drive your animals to drink, and the cost will be gradual. What do you say?"

The usual vociferous discussion ensued. Some thought the plan good; others opposed it. At last the government chief of the area stood up to speak.

"Men of Ngaarov," he said, "I think we do not need to do this thing. In a year or two the government will buy the pipe and bring it all the way to our homes without our having to work or sell our cattle."

These were the words the majority wished to hear, though some thought they had a hollow ring. But the uncertain half promise was more appealing than the hard, immediate reality. Denny's proposal was rejected.

"I knew the government would never do what the chief had suggested," he says reflectively, "and I realized that my time of usefulness was at an end. We had put a model in place and trained Maasai to operate and maintain it. The rest, I felt, would have to be left to them." Another unfinished project that Denny had long cherished was teaching the Maasai to put up hay for their livestock in preparation for droughts. Patiently, he explained how this was done in America each year, not only against dry seasons but also against the cold, barren winters when snow ("that funny white stuff you saw in the films we showed you") lay on the ground and prevented the cows from foraging. The elders were interested enough to help clear and fence a field, which, under irrigation, was soon deep in lush native grass while the surrounding plain was brown and dry. Unfortunately, the herd boys could not resist taking the fence down and driving their herds onto the good grass, a practice which the elders found more sensible than blameworthy. With a sigh, Denny abandoned the hay project, knowing that the Maasai were not ready for it.

Reviewing the achievements of fourteen years and projecting

what could still be done, he realized that for the people of Olosho-Oibor the motivation to strive further was blunted by the satisfaction of having at hand what they formerly lacked: ample supplies of water and food, their two most basic necessities. For many, the feeling was "What else is there? What more could we want?" So be it, he reasoned; we cannot push them farther than they wish to go. Their children will soon want more of what they see their neighboring tribes enjoying: jobs, cars, television sets. But those are not the things the Lord brought us here to help them get. Denny poured out his discouragements to Bruce Larson as the two men stood on the brink of a hill overlooking Larson Valley, so named by Denny in honor of the Seattle clergyman.

"You know, Bruce, some people have said that what Jeanne and I are doing out here is all wrong, that we shouldn't be meddling in these people's lives. I never paid any attention to that talk before, but maybe they're right. I sometimes wonder if our work here is really the Lord's will."

This was a new side of Denny, seldom revealed to anyone . . . Denny, the indomitable optimist, the stalwart positive thinker, expressing doubt. The pastor sensed in his friend's words a heart cry for affirmation. He pondered prayerfully before answering, then laid a hand on Denny's shoulder.

"Look down there, Denny," he suggested.

Below where they stood was a sprawling Maasai village, though an inexperienced eye could easily have failed to pick it out, so naturally did it blend with its surroundings. The mud-and-dung houses were nearly indistinguishable from large boulders, and only its shape differentiated the encircling thorn fence from the scrubby trees scattered about the valley floor.

"What you and Jeanne are doing," Dr. Larson said soberly, "is only the beginning of what needs to be done, and the entire process will take time. You must realize that you are not merely advancing their culture by a few years or even by a generation or two; you are lifting them over centuries. In response to the Lord's urging, you have helped them escape the deadly trap of cultural stagnation. You and Jeanne may not live to see the final result of all you have started, but it will happen, you may be sure! Children not yet born will benefit by what you have done. Their mothers will tell them of the White man and woman who cared enough about the Maasai people to come and live among them and bring them a better way of life."

Haunted at times by the fear that the results of their labors might vanish quickly when they left, the Grindalls nevertheless prepared to close this long chapter in the story of their lives. Samuel accepted responsibility for Denny's management role, with Jonathan as his trusted helper. Meticulously, Denny went over with them the thousand and one details they would need to oversee: operation, maintenance and repair of vehicles, tractors, pumps, generators and other equipment; monitoring the water level in the dams; cleaning the settling tanks and filters in the pipeline; making sure that the herdsmen did not allow their animals to trample the dams; planting, cultivating and irrigating the shamba; and so on, and so on and so on. Later, after returning to Seattle, Denny recorded detailed instructions on tapes and mailed them to Samuel. He also went over the necessary manual operations with three trusted young workmen: George, Mauora and Noah. Noah and Mauora were put in charge of the shamba, which involved not only the planting, cultivation, weeding and irrigating but also encouraging the other villagers to continue to work their individual garden plots. Mauora was also to keep an eye on the water tanks to be sure they were always filled. George was to care for the operation and maintenance of the windmills as well as backing up the other two in the garden area. George's assignment was especially critical, for windmills operating continually are subject to tremendous wear due to high wind pressure. The oil reservoir that lubricates the drive shaft must be kept filled, the brake set and locked when winds are dangerously high, and the leather plungers on the pump replaced from time to time. Also, the spring on the hillside must be cleaned out every six months to prevent clogging by grass and weeds. All other details must be monitored regularly. Issuing these instructions gave Denny an emotional wrench, for he realized how heavy the responsibilities were that he was placing on these young men.

Although Denny made no mention of his and Jeanne's impending departure, his three apprentices were acutely aware of the reason behind all the precise instructions they were receiving. Mauora, the youngest, who preferred to be called by his new Christian name, Jonathan, said sadly, "We know you go away, Simba. But you not stay away always. You come back and see us sometime, okay?"

As Denny and Jeanne busied themselves with the myriad of details of closing out fourteen years of work, they tried to do it as inconspicuously as possible, for they wished to avoid the emotional farewell they were sure their Maasai friends would insist on giving them. They were only partially successful, for it was impossible to disguise the purpose of the many trips they made to Samuel's house with articles they chose to leave behind. One day Denny and Samuel were delivering a truckload of beds and household equipment. Jonah was riding in the truck bed to keep articles from bouncing out on the rutted road. Samuel brought up the subject of the Grindalls' departure, saying that Jonah and the other people of the district wanted to give them a farewell party. Having anticipated this, Denny firmly rejected the scheme. Then he relented a trifle. Not trusting his command of Maa, which was only adequate for workaday purposes, he called on Samuel to interpret the thought that was on his heart. "Tell Jonah that I love him and thank him for all his help. Tell him he is my favorite of all the fellows who have helped me all these years. I remember that when we dug out the dam on the hillside, he gave up his own spring, the one the people recognized as his, for the sake of the others."

Samuel relayed the message. From the jolting truck bed, Jonah listened closely, then delivered a lengthy response, which Samuel translated.

"He says he did not ever think anyone would come here and do so many good things for his people. He is proud of learning to do so many things himself that he thought only White people could do. He says, 'Tell Simba I love him and will never forget him.' "

Denny smiled. "Tell him one more thing, Sam. Tell him I'm coming back some day to help him build his own house of latest American design."

During the Grindalls' final months in Kenya, the government land demarcation program began to be implemented. Among the more enlightened Maasai, those who were aware of what was happening, there was a predictable scramble for the choicest parcels of land. Chief Simeon, who was never one to overlook an opportunity to increase his wealth, cast a covetous eye on the ten-acre shamba that he knew would become available when Denny and Jeanne departed. Samuel acted quickly, though, pointing out to the government officials that the garden had always belonged to all the people and now, to ensure that it would remain so, it should go to MASI, which would continue to exist and operate under his direction. Much to Simeon's disappointment, this argument prevailed. Simeon began to murmur harsh words about Samuel, and some of these eventually came to Denny's ear. Upon hearing of them, Denny sought out the chief at once.

"Simeon," he said, "in my country there is an old fable about a man who found a starving dog. He took the dog into his home and fed him well until the dog regained his health. Then one day, for no reason, the dog bit the man's hand." He paused to let his words sink in. True Maasai that he was, the chief could not resist a story; he was listening closely.

"You are acting like that dog," Denny resumed sternly. "Everything Samuel has done here has been for the good of all the people, including you. Now when you go around saying bad things about him, you are behaving like the dog that bit the hand of the man who fed him." For once the greatest of all Maasai orators had nothing to say.

Denny and Jeanne live now in their beach cottage at Suquamish, Washington, a sleepy little town populated by a congenial mix of Indians and retirees. They enjoy a quiet but busy life. Denny trains homing pigeons, cuts firewood, cultivates a five-acre garden and sells hybrid berries of his own development to the local bakeries. Jeanne busies herself with their grandchildren and a host of domestic, church and civic activities. The Grindalls take the ferry to Seattle to maintain a continuing relationship with their beloved University Presbyterian Church, though they occasionally worship at nearby Rolling Bay. They keep in close contact with their Maasai friends, exchanging tapes with Samuel at least monthly. Recently they received the following letter from a young man they have known since his childhood:

Dear Denny and Jeanne,

I greet you in the name of our Lord Jesus Christ. *Sopa oling ama ira sopati . . . asi oling.* I do hope that you still remember the Maasai language. Is there cold in America now as here in Kenya? I know that you are busy always working in your shamba either in winter or in summer because a farmer never rests, and when he or she rests the whole world suffers from hunger. May our

Almighty Heavenly Father bless you as you continuing serving Him.

Now I really believe that your joy is full, because as you came to Kenya to serve the Lord and Maasai people you did a lot to convince them about the hidden truth from the gospel of our Lord Jesus Christ. You never despaired. You toiled day and night so that you may see the fruit of your mission. The seed you planted has now multiplied and spread all over Kajiado district. . . . Again the joy is that we now have six trained church ministers who are on their practicals to join the ministry. I, Stephen, is among the six. I always remember the words you said to us at Olosho-Oibor Dam by saying, "You young men wake up. Put down your blankets and big coats so you may work with your hands and also give light to your people." For this reason I would like to tell you that when great men pass away their good work and words never pass away. They will always have good reputations through all generations to come.

Well, I am doing well in my practical. I am almost finishing it, and I do hope that before the end of this year I will be ordained. My family is also doing well. They are not staying with me at Nyere. They are at home at Entosha. Three of my daughters are at school at Kimuka and the two are at home. I finished my course last year in November and started my practicals in January of this year. My prayer is that God to make way for me to be posted in Maasailand where the harvest is ready and big, with very few workers. Rev. Samuel Pulei is doing a lot to cover the whole area, you know, but the work is too much for him. According to my capacity of understanding, I really believe that if Samuel Pulei did not avail himself and resign from the African Church, and being paid by the head office and join you to serve my people, the Maasai work which is done in Maasailand would not have come up to the point where it is now. These things had taken place due to total sacrifice of both spirit, mind and body.

I have but very little to say by now because much to say cannot fit the paper. May God Almighty bless your souls and bodies as you continue serving Him and with Him. Convey my greetings to the members of your family and to the brethren of your parish.

Yours in Yesochristo,
Stephen Parmuat ole Mparinkoi

Epilog: Viewing the Miracle (February 1987)

Several weeks after I started writing this book, Denny informed me that he and Jeanne were planning to lead a group of MASI supporters on a combined Kenya safari and visit to Maasailand some nine months hence. He suggested that this would be a splendid opportunity for me to augment my research and offered to include reservations for my wife and me. This, I knew, was an opportunity of a lifetime; moreover, I had already begun to realize that attempting to write a book about Africa without seeing the place would call for audacity and imagination greater than I possessed. On the other hand, the timing, from my perspective, could not have been worse. The trip would occur in midwinter, a time I have for years reserved to do some technical editing for a valued client.

Denny's salesmanship, as the elders of Olosho-Oibor had found, was irresistible, and fortunately my client proved understanding. On a dazzling late winter day Betty and I joined twenty-six other excited travelers at the Vancouver (British Columbia) airport for the beginning of an adventure none of us will ever forget.

The Grindalls had compelling reasons for undertaking this odyssey. For the four years following their retirement, loyal supporters at the University Presbyterian Church had pressed to be taken for an on-site review of their MASI project. Also, the people of Olosho-Oibor had been urging the Grindalls to return for a reunion. And naturally Denny wanted to see that the dams, windmills, pipelines, gardens and other installations were being properly maintained, for some of the reports he had received from Samuel were disturbing. The most serious was of an incident at Ngarroj, where, despite Denny's repeated warnings, the men had allowed their cattle to trample the bank of the dam, with the inevitable result that an unusually heavy rain washed it out. Luckily, the only casualty was a drowned giraffe. Chastened, the men repaired the dam under Samuel's direction and promised to keep their cows off it in the future. But this report and others convinced Denny that a personal tour of inspection was in order.

A major consideration was the impending turnover of MASI to the African Church. The Grindalls felt it was time to relinquish all responsibility, as well as all MASI property, to local leadership, and the MASI board of directors concurred with their plan. Samuel was also looking forward to retirement. A great deal must be done to prepare for the formal transfer, which was scheduled for 1990.

As our KLM 747 approached Nairobi and began its descent, a huge red sun, newly risen out of the Indian Ocean, blazed in the cabin windows, giving us our first impression of Africa. The next came as we deplaned: among several thousand people milling about the busy terminal, we were the only Whites! The Maasai people waiting to welcome us were readily distinguishable by their colorful robes and decorative ear ornaments. Spotting Denny and Jeanne, they went wild. After half an hour of raucous greeting, the hugs, handshakes and "sobas" diminished enough to allow us to escape to our hotel, the stately old Fairview.

Following a ten-day safari through Kenya's splendid game parks, we again made contact with our Maasai friends. On the rim of the Rift escarpment, at the very place where the Grindalls and Andersons had picnicked nineteen years earlier, we had our first glimpse of Maasailand. As we gazed across that vast, primordial plain, the

Rift Valley wind streamed against our faces, threatening to blow away our hats and eyeglasses. Our four vans carried us down into the valley to Pulei Village, where another noisy welcome awaited us.

It is impossible to exaggerate the exuberant joy that these warm-hearted people displayed; it spoke volumes about their appreciation and would have impressed even the Grindalls' harshest critics. As the hubbub gradually subsided, we were ushered to the nearby *alelacei,* where we were to share in a picnic. Two Maasai women, one carrying a pitcher and the other a basin, invited us to wash our hands as they moved past the benches where we were seated. Two men carved a goat, which the women then served. Samuel asked the blessing after first inviting any of the Maasai men who objected to eating in the presence of women to take their food apart from the group. None acted on this suggestion. Chief Simeon, attired in rubber boots and a faded raincoat despite the clear sky and eighty-degree temperature, delivered in Maa a stirring welcome to all of us and a tribute to the Grindalls, which Samuel interpreted into English for our benefit. Simeon said, "I wish I could make Denny young again so he could return and build more churches here."

With Tim Fairman, our Young Life representative, interpreting, I chatted with Jonah. He told me about having once killed a lion that had attacked one of his cows. As I pondered what it would be like to kill a hungry lion with a spear, my respect for Maasai courage soared. Then Samuel Nakeel took me for a tour of the old village nearby, where a handful of unreconstructed Maasai still dwelt. My tame suburban world seemed very far away.

In nearby Larson Valley we visited another old-style village. As our group and several village men listened, Denny conversed soberly with Stephen, a teen-age son of the chief. "Remember, Stephen," he said, laying his hand on the boy's shoulder. "You need to do just three things to have a successful life: trust God, love people . . . and have hope." Stephen nodded grave agreement at the first two admonitions but looked doubtful at the third. "It is very hard," he said softly.

The next day, Sunday, we worshiped outdoors at Olooseos with several hundred Maasai, many of whom were dressed in Western garb. The event was historic in two respects: for the first time in that district, eight Maasai men and one woman were ordained as church elders; and a very large group of women, numbering perhaps fifty, were initiated into the Women's Guild, an active and dedicated community service organization. My camcorder captured the joy on the women's faces and in their voices as they sang while colorful blue kerchiefs, the badge of membership, were tied around the heads of the initiates. Throughout the service the Rift wind swayed the tall, graceful gum trees that Denny had planted many years ago. There were speeches by African Church officials and a response by Dr. Bruce Larson of our group. One of the women of the Women's Guild delivered the sermon. The entire service lasted three and a half hours, yet none of the Maasai showed the slightest bit of restlessness.

After lunch at Samuel and Edith Pulei's home, Denny led the hardier souls among us on a tour of Chamness Lake and the site of the original dam high in the Ngong Hills. Several Maasai men and boys accompanied us. The lake, even though only half full after a long drought, was an impressive site in its arid setting. As we ascended the rugged slope, I experienced the incredible wait-a-bit bush (a row of blood spots suddenly appeared on my sleeve!). Near one of the faucets in the pipeline we saw bright-colored laundry drying on the low shrubs. Not far from the ruins of the concrete watering trough (battered to pieces by vandals), two of Chief Simeon's innumerable sons guarded a herd of goats. A couple of graceful Maasai maidens watched us from a ridge above our path.

As I panted along in pursuit of the indefatigable Denny, trying to catch his explanations on my camcorder, I noticed that Don Deibert, an engineer member of our party, was engaged in conversation with a Maasai lad of twelve or thirteen. They were discussing Archimedes' principle, which obviously meant more to the boy than to me. From this and other indications, we discovered that education is highly valued now, especially among the young people.

On the day before our departure I finally managed to interview Samuel. He and Denny had been so busy going over the many technical and administrative details on Denny's agenda that I had begun to fear that I would never get this rare opportunity. As we lounged comfortably on the broad lawn of the Fairview, with birds in countless numbers singing in the trees overhead and my tape recorder tracking our conversation, he told me the astounding story of the ordeal in his infancy, which of course he could only know from what his mother and others told him later. He showed me the scars on his chest where the old laibon had released the "evil spirits." Our conversation ranged across many tribes and nations and centuries of history. I marveled at his fund of knowledge and the quiet strength of his spirit. He spoke realistically, but confidently, about his expectations for the future of his people. He is convinced that those who have experienced the wholesome life that the Grindalls introduced will never revert to their old tribal patterns, and others will inevitably follow their example.

At the conclusion of our interview he presented me with a beautiful beaded belt of Maasai design. I was happy to be able to reciprocate with a gift for Samuel, a silver pocket compass that my father gave me long ago.

Surely, I concluded as we shook hands in parting, the uniting of this Maasai pastor with Denny and Jeanne Grindall must have been, as Samuel himself once said, "just a miracle."